GOD'S WORD:
MY GUARANTEE

UNLEASHING THE
POWER OF GOD'S WORD IN YOUR LIFE

"Then said the LORD unto me, 'Thou
hast well seen: for I will hasten my Word
to perform it'" (Jeremiah 1:12).

I present to you *God's Word: My Guarantee* with
my prayer that the Holy Spirit will use it to speak
timeless truth to your heart in a fresh, and new way.

RICHARD ONEBAMOI

THE ROCK
PUBLISHING

**The ROCK Publishing
Brussels**

Unless otherwise indicated, all Scripture quotations are taken from the King James Version of the Bible. Italics in Scripture are for emphasis only.

GOD'S WORD: MY GUARANTEE - UNLEASHING THE POWER OF GOD'S WORD IN YOUR LIFE

Copyright@2018 by Richard Onebamoi
ISBN 978-9-0812-6366-5

Richard Onebamoi International
P.O. Box 30
1200 Brussels
Belgium

E-mail: info@richardonebamoi.com
Websites: www.richardonebamoi.com; www.livingstoneworld.org; www.livingstoneworld.tv

Published by The ROCK **Publishing**
P.O. Box 30
1200 Brussels
Belgium

Printed in Belgium

CONTENTS

DEDICATION

I wish to dedicate this book to my Heavenly Father, God, for the privilege of being His useable vessel and to my Redeemer, Jesus Christ, the Author and the Finisher of my faith.

To the Holy Spirit, the Pillar of cloud by day and the Pillar of fire by night, who has continually helped me to understand that God's Word is my ultimate guarantee.

It is my privilege to dedicate this book to my parents-in-law, Baba Thomas and Mama Tryphosa Kizigha. You both are an amazing Mum and Dad, as you both have significantly touched lives with your love, passion, and integrity.

Thanks for raising an exceptional daughter to whom I am privileged to be married.

ACKNOWLEDGMENT

I wish to express my gratitude to my Heavenly Father, God, for giving me the privilege to become a suitable vessel in His hand and sincerely acknowledge the sacrificial contributions of the following:

My beloved wife, Catherine K. Onebamoi, and my precious children, Naomi-Lisha, Nearia-Destinie, Nathania-Mia, and Nathan-Richard Jr., whose births have made me forever grateful to God for the opportunity to be a caretaker.

Apostle Warren & Pastor LaCatherine Martin, my yoke friends, and co-workers in the Lord's vineyard, and the entire Miracle Temple of Christ International family for your love and prayers.

Pastors Julius & Lovett Isibor, my yoke friends and co-workers in the Lord's vineyard, and the entire International Christian Center family for your friendship, love, and encouragement.

Pastor Don & Prophetess Dennett Strickland, whom I have come to love and admire especially. Thank you for your love and hospitality.

Pastor Zelma Marcella Boone for your dedication and service to the Lord. You are a gem of inestimable value. Keep up the excellent work!

To all the beautiful vessels of God who have been sources of great inspiration and encouragement and from whom I have learned a great deal over the years.

May God truly and richly bless you all.

WHAT PEOPLE ARE SAYING ABOUT
GOD'S WORD: MY GUARANTEE

"The Word of God has stood the tests of time, scrutiny and skeptics. In a world of fast changes, only one thing is steadfast to be the sure foundation for life, and that is the Word of Almighty God. As you peruse the pages of this book penned by Apostle Richard Onebamoi, your hope will be stirred, and your faith will be anchored to appropriate what rightfully belongs to you. God's Word is God speaking to you. Apostle Richard has put into your lap a masterpiece handbook for victory. Read it and lay hold of the high life that the Word has made available to you. The truths unveiled in this book will enable you to display the divine nature that is inside of you." - *Dr. Glenn Arekion, Author: Seven Ways To Increase Your Anointing*
Conference speaker

"With prophetic surgical precision, Apostle Richard Onebamoi crafts a kingdom roadmap for any believer who desires the aura of perpetual victory to patronize their life and ministry. In his exemplary book "God's Word My Guarantee," he demonstrates both the superiority and infallibility of the Word of God as the preamble to any kind of Manifest Destiny. This is a book that every leader and laity alike will find essential. I highly recommend this well researched apostolic work." - *Dr. Francis Myles, Author: The Order of Melchizedek, Senior Pastor: Lovefest Church International, Scottsdale, Arizona, USA*

"First and foremost, I'll like to express my profound love and appreciation to the author of this book, Apostle Richard Onebamoi for the honor and privilege to write an endorsement for his latest book, God's Word: My Guarantee.

This book is a significant teaching and inspirational manual filled with godly principles that can guarantee success in the lives of those who put them into practice. I also believe that everyone who read through the pages will find it very relevant and applicable to the different situations they face in life.

Apostle Richard Onebamoi has skilfully with all simplicity put together a training manual for anyone who has a strong desire to see God use them in the work of the ministry, especially in the current world climate of hopelessness. According to him, God's Word is your life, your faith, your source of strength, and your anchor." I agree with him.

I strongly believe that this book will inspire and stir up the faith of many people for a breakthrough, especially people who for so long have been longing to rise above certain areas of limitations they have encountered. Those who capture and apply the biblical principles of these pages of revelation will see the dawning of a New day in their Christian life.

It gives me great pleasure to highly recommend this book for your reading. Be blessed as you read it in Jesus name!" - *Bishop Paul Fadeyi, General Overseer, Grace Outreach Church, Dartford, Kent, UK*

"In a world of conflicting voices, Rev. Onebamoi, a passionate expositor of the Bible, calls on believers to fall back in love with the word of God, and to study the Holy Scriptures, for more significant insights, a stronger faith, and a closer walk with God. The subject of this book is highly timely." - *Emmanuel Idu, Apostle/General Overseer, Winners Church International*

"God's Word: My Guarantee is a Bible handbook filled with such depth and practicality that it will help you go through the meanders of life with such a great understanding of the Word of God already made available for you to win. The Word will always work if you work it." - *Dr. Freddy P S Olela, President and Founder, Joshua Generation Ministries*

"In this new and timely book, Dr. Richard Onebamoi clearly unleashes in-depth revelations capable of turning any man's life around!

I highly recommend this book to any serious minded individual in these last days when many people are just running after prophecies and signs. This book is a FOUNDATIONAL MASTERPIECE to keep one free from error, deception and falling away. Plus to keep one rooted and grounded in truth, success and constant victory. It's A must read." - *Apostle Chris Lordhills Akaolisa, Global President, Treasures of Faith Ministries International, South Africa.*

"In this powerful work, "God's Word: My Guarantee," Dr. Onebamoi skillfully expounds and reveals the power and potency of God's Word in our lives. He masterfully guides the reader into aligning themselves with the Living Word and confessing the Rhema to see supernatural results. If you are serious about walking in the Supernatural and taking your life to the next level, this book is for you. Carefully read and consider the divine instruction within these pages, and your life will never be the same!" - *Dr. Kynan Bridges, Bestselling Author of 90 Days of Power Prayer, Senior Pastor, Grace & Peace Global Fellowship, Inc., www.kynanbridges.com*

"Apostle Richard has brought great attention to the importance of the Word of God in victorious Christian living. He has given a roadmap on how to use the Word of God effortlessly.

Studiously well researched and written, the presentation is clear and well reasoned out. This book will help the readers anchor themselves in the finality and heavy weight of the Word of God.

I am refreshed and encouraged that this book will re-focus the Body of Christ on the relevance of the application of the Word of God To every aspect of our lives.

I enjoyed the spread and range of the numerous chapters showcasing the author's deep exposure to the Word of God as a Pastor and Apostle.

His style is easy to read and understand and apply. I congratulate Dr. Richard and his team for an outstanding job. Thank you and more grace, Sir." - *Apostle Chuzzy Udewa, Glory House World Church, Atlanta*

"In a generation where lots of noise is coming from the City, we need to be able to hear the Voice from the Temple. In this expansive and comprehensive book on the Word of God, Dr. Onebamoi has provided an A-Z of operating in and profiting from the Word. Because in the last days, the counterfeit making machine of the enemy will be vastly improved, we need to be able to know the Word of God to us in every situation to avoid making a shipwreck of our faith. This book is highly recommended as a must read for any Christian who wants to be schooled in understanding the Word of God, how to personalize the Word and to transcend the distractions of this Age to become doers of the Word. This is a detailed book that will form one of my best read on the subject of operating by the Word, and I commend the author for an awesome and profound contribution to the Kingdom at such a time as this. Blessings always." - *Dr. Charles Omole, Winning Faith Outreach, United Kingdom*

"I am privileged and honored to endorse Dr. Richard Onebamoi, God's Word My Guarantee. This book contains a timely message and will encourage many people to walk and live by the Word of God. The Word of God remained the only true and tested revelation of God and HIs operation, anything outside the Word of God practiced whether in church or any religious circles is nothing but deception. The Word of God reveals God, His attributes and method of His operation which the church can not afford to be ignorant of.

Dr. Richard is a great exegetical preacher of the Word. He has a unique way of delivering the Word which includes information, illumination and very inspirational.

Dr. Richard over the years has been faithful to his calling as a teacher of the Word even when many have chosen to teach what cannot be validated by the written Word because of fame.

I highly recommend this book as it a timely book that will become a manual for the preservation of the church and its foundational truths." - *Bishop Dr. AM Mwami, Devoted Ambassadors For Christ Ministries (President), Holy Ghost Fire House Worldwide (Senior Pastor), Greater Faith School of World Missions (Director), Logos University Mbombela Chapter (Representative), International Faith Fellowship of Ministers and Churches (Chairman)*

FORWARD

Apostle Richard ONEBAMOI has captured the essence and importance of God's Word as it relates to a believer in Christ. *God's Word: My Guarantee* is a clear and concise book that illuminates the treasures of God's promises.

The Body of Christ is facing mediocrity, stagnation, and apostasy at unprecedented levels with only spurts of revival now and again. The book *God's Word: My Guarantee* surfaces at the right time to help empower the Church and re-establish God's principles as articulated in the Word of God.

In this book, Apostle Onebamoi is used by God as a catalyst to enable the believer to prepare for the "all saints move of God" in these last days. I highly recommend this book to *every* believer.

Apostle Warren D. Martin, SR.
Miracle Temple of Christ Int'l
Davenport, FL
USA

NOTE

The principal purpose of words is communication; hence, throughout this book, I felt it pertinent and essential to use several versions of Scriptures, Hebrew, and Greek text, for easy comprehension and more also, to enable you to get more out of the Bible when you read different translations of the same passage.

INTRODUCTION

G od's Word is a treasure of immeasurable value with declarations of His will, purpose, and principles to man. God's Word serves as a catalyst that can propel and enable you to function and fulfill your God-given destinies as you seek to advance God's plans and purposes on earth.

God's Word is an indispensable, comprehensive resource for equipping men, and in turn, making them competent for His service. In ancient and present times, God's Word has always been and still is the final arbiter for man. The patriarchs of old trusted God's Word in moments of small and significant victories as well as in moments of despair. In the same way, the Church today is also admonished to trust in God's unfailing Word in stable and uncertain times.

Today, man has seen technological advancement in some way beyond possible human description, thus, making reliance on God and His Word all the more difficult. The momentum of development has been so alarming that it has resulted in immeasurable success but at the same time unendurable pressure in various aspects of life.

This situation has created an inconceivable dilemma that has plagued humanity, thus, producing hunger and a search for someone or something that has the adeptness to guarantee stability, consistency, and solve the numerous problems with which one is confronted. As a result of this incongruous situation, man seems to have tried everything possible to seek the powers that be in an attempt to find solutions to his predicaments and answers to the numerous unanswered questions in his heart.

It is without a shred of doubt that God's Word is our final arbiter in the times we live in, human potential and man's achievements notwithstanding. It is imperative to note that in spite of man's increase in scientific, medical and technological knowledge and its continued growth at an astronomical pace, the issues that plague humanity have not been alleviated; they've rather been exacerbated in many instances.

Uncertainty and despair continue to drive man to the point of confusion and exhaustion. On the contrary, God's Word stands out as the only remedy for human maladies and the principal instrument for man's salvation.

Countless numbers of people have had the privilege to experience God's Word as their final and ultimate guarantee in the face of imminent danger, despair, and discouragement. God's Word declares, *"For I will hasten my Word to perform it"* (Jeremiah 1:12). I am convinced, beyond any reasonable doubt, that that which God has spoken concerning you, He will perform above what you think or imagine according to His power that works within you.

It is my humble belief that in the pages of this book, *God's Word: My Guarantee,* you will locate a word that will radically revolutionize your thinking and thrust you toward finding solace and reason to trust God's Word as the final authority and arbiter for your life and actions as you gravitate toward your finish line.

I prayerfully recommend this book to you, your family, and your ministries. It will enhance your understanding of and confidence in God's Word, as your ultimate guarantee, and you will learn to unleash the power of God's Word in your life and do exploits for God.

Richard ONEBAMOI

CHAPTER 1

THE AUTHORITY OF GOD'S WORD

GOD'S WORD:
INSPIRED REVELATION OF GOD

. . . .

"All scripture is given by inspiration of God and is profitable for doctrine, for reproof, for correction, for instruction in righteousness: That the man of God may be perfect, thoroughly furnished unto all good works" (King James Version, 2 Timothy 3: 16-17).

"All Scripture is inspired by God and is useful to teach us what is true and to make us realize what is wrong in our lives. It corrects us when we are wrong and teaches us to do what is right. God uses it to prepare and equip his people to do every good work." (New Living Translation, 2 Timothy 3: 16-17).

"All Scripture is inspired by God and profitable for teaching, for reproof, for correction, for training in righteousness; so that the man of God may be

1

adequate, equipped for every good work" (New American Standard, 2 Timothy 3: 16-17).

"All Scripture is God-breathed [given by divine inspiration] and is profitable for instruction, for conviction [of sin], for correction [of error and restoration to obedience], for training in righteousness [learning to live in conformity to God's will, both publicly and privately—behaving honorably with personal integrity and moral courage]; so that the man of God may be complete and proficient, outfitted and thoroughly equipped for every good work" (Amplified Bible, 2 Timothy 3: 16-17).

The Bible is God's revealed will. God's inspired Word and the eternal God are one. The inspiration of Scripture as God's Word affirms its authority and infallibility because it was written under the leading and guidance of the Holy Spirit, thus, making God the author of the Bible.

Consequently, the Scriptures are free from all error of fact or principle or teachings. God's Word is the final authority for all of humanity. Whether we recognize the power of the Scriptures or not, the fact remains that God is the author of the Bible and in this lies the authority of God's Word (the Bible).

In the above passage of Scripture, the Greek word translated *"inspiration of God"* is *Theópneustos* (Strong's G2315), a compound word that comprises *Theós* (Strong's G2316) meaning *"God"* and *Pnéō* (Strong's G4154) meaning *"to breathe," "to breathe out."* The inspiration of God, therefore, implies "God-breathed." Simply put, the Bible is not written by the will of man, neither is it humanity's conceptualism or his attempt to diagnose or philosophize God, but rather the product of divine activity and the means by which God reveals Himself and declares His plans and purposes to man.

Erich Sauer, a German theologian, stated about inspiration: "Biblical inspiration ... is that activity of the Holy Spirit through which He mysteriously filled the human spirit of the Biblical writers and guided them and overruled them, so that there arose an infallible, Spirit-wrought writing, a sacred record, a Book of God, with which the Spirit of God evermore organically unites Himself." The Scriptures are not the words or thoughts of mere men, but of Spirit-guided men who spoke and wrote the very Word of God. Second Peter 1:20-21 elaborates this truth, saying that no prophecy of the Scripture is of any private interpretation.

Inspiration is the in-breathing of God into the minds of human writers, thus, enabling them to write the Word of God. The Bible, therefore, is not a dead book: it is alive, it is inspired. It is as much the Word of God as if He spoke every single word of it with His mouth. The Holy Spirit further emphasizes the integrity of God's Word and attests to the inspiration of the Scriptures through Peter when he says, *"Knowing this first, that no prophecy of the scripture is of any private interpretation. For the prophecy came not in old time by the will of man: but holy men of God spake as they were moved by the Holy Ghost"* (2 Peter 1:20-21). So holy men wrote as the Holy Spirit inspired them. Period!

The Bible declares,

> *"And the Lord God formed man of the dust of the ground, and breathed into his nostrils the breath of life; and man became a living soul"* (Genesis 2:7).

In the light of the Scripture above, when God breathed into Adam's nostrils, he became a living soul; he had the very life of God on the inside of him. In the same manner, God also breathed the breath of life into human vessels as conduits through whom His Word was written. He inspired and communicated His Word to the writers as the Holy Spirit moved upon them. It suffices to say, therefore, that God is the author of the Bible.

> *"By the Word of the Lord were the heavens made; and all the host of them by the breath of his mouth. He gathereth the waters of the sea together as an heap: he layeth up the depth in storehouses. Let all the*

earth fear the Lord: let all the inhabitants of the world
stand in awe of him. For he spake, and it was done;
he commanded, and it stood fast" (Psalms 33:6-9).

God is the power of His Word. As we examine this passage of Scripture above, we see the power of the Word of God in operation; He made the heavens and all that it contains. The authority of God's Word is demonstrated as we gaze at creation and everything around us. What we see and experience is the expression of the authority and power of the Word of God.

Genesis 1:1-1 reads: *"In the beginning, God created the heaven and the earth."* Furthermore, God created the heavens and the earth by the instrumentality of His Word; He said, and it was so. God's Word carries as much authority and creative power today as it did then, and that same authority and power are still available and operative for us as we engage and take advantage of the authority and power in the Word of God.

Prophet Jeremiah explained, *"Then said the Lord unto me, 'Thou hast well seen: for I will hasten my word to perform it"* (Jeremiah 1:12). The word *"perform"* comes from the Hebrew word *Asah* (Strong's H6213*)*, which means, *"to do," "to fashion," "to accomplish," "to make," "to act with effect."* God's Word for your life will not go unattended, for God watches over His Word to do and accomplish it. He will make good what He has promised in His Word concerning us.

The NIV rendering of Jeremiah 1:12 states, *"The LORD said to me, 'You have seen correctly, for I am watching to see that my word is fulfilled.'"* The Almighty God watches His Word to see to its fulfillment. Hence, you can rely on God's Word as the final arbiter and your ultimate guarantee in all matters of life.

God's Word is so authoritative that the entire universe was created, was made to operate, and was held in place by the word of His power (see Hebrews 1:3). Inherent in God's Word is the ability to regenerate. First Peter 1:23 reads: *"Being born again, not of corruptible seed, but of incorruptible, by the word of God, which liveth and abideth forever."* The Word of God is the incorruptible seed out of which divine nature is produced in us. You can rest assured that the Scripture cannot be broken, canceled, or annulled for it will deliver all that it is meant to create in our lives.

The Word of God is alive and active and therefore produces results. Hebrews 4:12 reads: *"For the word of God is quick, and powerful, and sharper than any two-edged sword, piercing even to the dividing asunder of soul and spirit, and of the joints and marrow, and is a discerner of the thoughts and intents of the heart."* The degree of the working of the Word of God in any man depends on how he receives and attends to the Word of God. That is, God's Word is operative in the believer as they respond to it in its application by faith.

The Bible is God's Word, living and the absolute Truth. The Scriptural passage of 2 Timothy 3: 16-17 lets us understand that God divinely inspires all Scripture. It is profitable for doctrine, it is beneficial for reproof, it is advantageous for correction, and it is valuable for instruction in righteousness to the end that the child of God will be perfect and thoroughly furnished for good works (see Deuteronomy 4:10).

These Scriptural texts further settle the fact that God's Word is not a set of human assumptions and probabilities but a sure word of prophecy from God (2 Peter 1:19).

> *"The grass withereth, the flower fadeth: but the word of our God shall stand forever"* (Isaiah 40:8).

The authority of God's Word is also predicated on the fact that God's Word is infallible, for as it was written under the guidance of the Holy Spirit; it is, therefore, free from all error and deteriorations of facts. The Bible is the authentic, authoritative, reliable *Word of God.* In all matters with which it deals. *"Men and brethren, this scripture must needs have been fulfilled, which the Holy Ghost by the mouth of David spake before concerning Judas, which was guide to them that took Jesus"* (Acts 1:16). It is written freely by its authors but it is so in-breathed by the Holy Spirit that it is correctly and accurately documented and it instructs us in the will of God.

As the divinely inspired Word, the Bible gives us God's perspective on how we should live. It represents God's way of thinking; for that reason, God's Word is His very essence. The Scripture is true and infallible in all that it affirms and is dependable and supremely authoritative in all matters of faith, personal life, and conduct. Hence, the Gospel of Matthew elucidates that man does not live by bread alone but by every Word that proceeds out of the mouth of God (see Matthew 4:4).

The Bible is not a book of abstract speculations about God; instead, it is a living book because it contains the Living Word of the Living God, the Maker of the heavens and the earth. Also, the Bible is an analysis of history. It describes God's Words and actions and what those efforts mean to the people of God. The Word of God is immutable; it's unbreakable (John 10:35); God's Word is the source of faith (Romans 10:17). It shall never pass away (Matthew 24:35), and it shall abide forever (1 Peter 1:23).

John 10:35b reads: *"...And the scripture cannot be broken."* The authority of the Scripture is final; it *cannot be set aside.*

THE PURPOSE OF THE WORD

. . . .

"All scripture is given by inspiration of God, and is profitable for doctrine, for reproof, for correction, for instruction in righteousness" (2 Timothy 3:16).

God is a God of purpose and objectivity. Whatever God declares or does has significance. In the text aforementioned, the purpose of God's Word is evident. This shows that the Word of God provides the authoritative instruction of faith and behavior, conviction of sin when we fail, what is needed to restore us to an inculpable state and teaches right living.

The Word of God is authoritative and powerful and is useful for:

- **Doctrine:** The word *"doctrine"* is the Greek word *"Didaskalía,"* (Strong's G1319) meaning "learning," "that which is taught," or "teaching." Doctrine, therefore, is the act of teaching or communicating instructions and that which is taught. God's Word is authoritative and useful for explaining the principles of God.

- **Reproof:** The Greek word for *"reproof"* is *"Élenchos"* (Strong's G1650), and it means "conviction," "reproof," or "rebuke." The Word of God brings rebuke, not with the intent of destroying us but to set us on the right path in our dealings with God and man. Now and then we tend to go astray, and God's Word is useful in administering reproof to convince us of the truth in order to bring us back in the right direction

- **Correction**: The word *"correction"* is the Greek word *"Epanórthsis"* (Strong's G1882), a compound word that comprises *Epi* (Strong's G1909) meaning "to" and *Anorthoo* (Strong's G461) meaning "a straightening up again." Epanórthsis, therefore, implies a straightening up again or rectification, a setting to right, reparation, or restoration to an upright or right state. We often tend to resist correction when it comes from someone else. The implication is that the Scriptures are a potent resource for bringing corrections into our lives and the proper condition regarding morals when we are missing the mark. Who can argue with God's Word?

- **Instruction:** The word *"instruction"* is the Greek word *"Paideía"* (Strong's G3809). It is in the process of instruction in which we are taught what is right and what is required of us so that we may lead a holy life. God's Word serves this purpose. Every significant breakthrough in Scripture can be traceable to obeyed instructions. As we are instructed, we glean wisdom and principles from God's Word that shows us how to lead an upright life.

Moreover, all this is done in righteousness that we may have a right standing with God.

CHAPTER 2

THE DIMENSIONS OF GOD'S WORD

God's Word subsists in three forms or realms, yet they are inseparable and in harmony with one another:

- The Living Word of God
- The Written Word of God
- The Spoken Word of God

The Living Word of God

"In the beginning was the Word, and the Word was with God, and the Word was God" (John 1:1).

The Word *"ho lógos"* was in the beginning, the Word *"ho lógos"* was with God, and the Word *"ho lógos"* was God. This is Jesus Christ in His pre-incarnate state, also known as *ho lógos* (Strong's G3056) *(*The Word), presenting Him as the second personality of the Godhead who is the exact imprint of God's nature, the external expression of divine intelligence and the manifestation of divine essence.

The Scripture helps us understand that The Word is the brightness of God's Glory and the express image of His person: in other words, the exact expression of God's essence or nature, the self-revealing characteristics and the embodiment of Elohim (see Hebrews 1:3).

The Written Word of God

> *"All scripture is given by inspiration of God, and is profitable for doctrine, for reproof, for correction, for instruction in righteousness"* (2 Timothy 3:16).

These are the writings of men that were inspired and carried along by the Spirit of God who enabled them to accurately document the truthful record of what God wants us to know and do. In 2 Peter 1:20-21, Apostle Peter declares: *"Knowing this first, that no prophecy of the scripture is of any private interpretation. For the prophecy came not in old time by the will of man: but holy men of God spake as they were moved by the Holy Ghost."* The Scripture makes it clear that God's Word is dependable because it has a divine source and is not of human origin, for men were moved by the Holy Spirit as they wrote the Word of God. For this reason, we can rely on it as our ultimate guarantee in all matters of life. God's Word has never failed, and it will never fail.

The Spoken Word of God

> *"Death and life are in the power of the tongue: and they that love it shall eat the fruit thereof"* (Proverbs 18:21).

God created man in His image, after His likeness and gave man complete authority over all of His creation (see Genesis 1:26). Thus, the man was created in the very likeness of God Himself. Just as God has the power to speak and create things from His spoken words, we too have been given the ability to speak and create through our words.

The Word of God, spoken in faith in the name of Jesus, has the awesome power to overcome seemingly insurmountable impediments. This is God by His Holy Spirit speaking His counsel into the hearts of men. Such speaking comes in various forms. For example, it may come as a still, small voice in one's spirit during moments of Bible studies, times of prayer and meditation, or during the preaching of God's Word. When God's Word is spoken, heard, and acted upon, it impacts us and deals with particular circumstances or needs in our lives. There is inherent divine power in the Word of God that brings about spiritual and physical results in our lives when received and acted upon by faith (see 1 Thessalonians 2:13).

RHEMA AND LOGOS

There are two different Greek words used to describe the Word of God in the Bible, which are *Lógos* (Strong's G3056) and *Rhēma* (Strong's G4487), respectively. The Greek word *Lógos* refers to the total utterance of God, which is the complete revelation of what God has said. On the other hand, *Rhēma* is distinct from *lógos* in that it does not refer to the Bible as a whole. Instead, it relates to a specific saying of God, verse or portion of Scripture, which applies exclusively to a particular situation, to a revelation, word, or insight from God, which the Holy Spirit brings to our attention.

Ephesians 6:17 reads, *"And take the helmet of salvation, and the sword of the Spirit, which is the Word of God."* Thus, *Rhema* is the *revealed Word of God.* A single promise or promises that the Holy Spirit quickens in your heart from God's Word, when faced with a situation, need, trial or difficulty, becomes the *Rhema* Word, the "now word," for you in that specific case.

When you receive this *Rhēma* Word, (a now word of promise), you know that God is speaking a personal word to you by His Spirit, regarding something on your heart or a situation in your life. Whether it is *Lógos* revelation of God's Word, (the total inspired Word of God) or *Rhēma*, a quickened word from the written Word of God to you in moments of personal meditation or the spoken word, God's Word is still your ultimate guarantee in all situations and circumstances and powerful in its workings. When God quickens a *Rhēma* Word, a verse or verses that you have read many times before suddenly take on a new meaning, and you can see how they apply to a specific situation or need for direction in your life. As this *Rhēma,* that is verse or portion of Scriptures that the Holy Spirit illuminates, settles in your spirit; miraculous things begin to happen.

First Epistle to the Thessalonian Church reads: *"For this cause also thank we God without ceasing, because, when ye received the word of God which ye heard of us, ye received it not as the word of men, but as it is in truth, the word of God, which effectually worketh also in you that believe"* (1 Thessalonians 2:13). The Greek word for *"effectually worketh"* is *Energéō* (Strong's G1754), which denotes "to be operative," "to be at work," "to put forth power," "to be active" "powerful in action." This implies that the power to perform and the fulfillment of God's Word do not lie in man or anything that he possesses, but lie in the burden-removing, yoke-destroying power of God inherent in His Word.

Apostle Paul elucidates that the Word of God is not an insignificant word of man. God is the source and power of both *Lógos* and *Rhēma* Word. Consequently, this makes the Word of God authentic and authoritative. God's Word possesses an inherent ability that works in and through those who adhere to, trust in, and rely on it. For without doubt or fear, you can depend entirely on God's Word as your ultimate guarantee in all areas of your life. God's Word is so authoritative and active that it will not return void until it has accomplished the purpose and prospers in that for which it was sent (see Isaiah 55:10-11). God and His Word cannot be separated, for God and His Word are one.

Furthermore, the Bible declares, *"Power belongeth unto God"* (Psalms 62:11). Consequently, the power to accomplish His Word is inherent in His Word. The Scriptures let us understand that *"God is not a man that he should lie; neither the son of man that he should repent: hath he said, and shall he not do it? Or hath he spoken, and shall he not make it good?"* (Numbers 23:19). Whatever God's intents are, when spoken out of His mouth, they are exactly what they become. For instance, if God's intention is light, when He says, "Let there be light," there will be light. If God's Word declares you are healed, you are healed. If it states you are blessed, you are blessed.

You have to recognize that no matter how high the mountain or how low the valley you are confronted with is, God stays faithful to His Word. He neither lies nor repents but makes all things right on your behalf and perfects all that concerns you (see Psalms 138:8). Consequently, your confidence in God's Word should not be shaken, for God is able and will perform His Word and make it useful in your life.

God's Word is eternally efficacious; you must learn to believe, appropriate it and hold onto that which He has spoken and it shall come to pass if you do not faint. It is of utmost importance to reiterate that the Word of God works if only you can believe and hold tenaciously to it without wavering. Apostle James observes that no man that is double-minded and unstable in his ways can or should expect to receive anything from God (see James 1:6-8).

At every level of our growth and development, God's Word is invaluable; whether you are new to the faith or a veteran in the faith, the Word of God has relevance to your growth and spiritual wellbeing.

Water Dimension of God's Word: God's Word is often referred to as water in Scriptures because it serves as a cleansing agent. Apostle Paul stated: *"That he might sanctify and cleanse it with the washing of water by the word"* (Ephesians 5:26-27). Water is here used as the symbol of the cleansing and purifying power of the Word of God. This is what Apostle Paul described when he wrote concerning Jesus' cleansing of the Church. Hence, water in the Scriptures signifies the cleanup of the sinner by the washing of the water of the Word of God. It is vital that we engage in this dimension of the Word of God daily in enjoying its purifying effect upon our lives.

Furthermore, Titus 3:5 reads, *"Not by works of righteousness which we have done, but according to his mercy he saved us, by the washing of regeneration, and renewing of the Holy Ghost."* This dimension of God's Word makes us pure and holy by operating in our hearts, conscience, thoughts, and actions, and thereby bringing in a new life from God to be accomplished by the instrumentality of the truth, which is the Word of God (see John 17:1).

Milk Dimension of God's Word: First Peter 2:2 reads, *"As newborn babes, desire the sincere milk of the word, that ye may grow thereby."* The word *milk* in the above text is the Greek word *Gála* (Strong's G1051), meaning the basic, elemental teachings of true Christianity first learned by new believers. Our spiritual growth is contingent on desiring and taking in the milk of God's Word. When a child is newly born, the child is fed with milk, which contains essential nutrients that it needs to grow to become strong and mature. Likewise, when born again, we ought to be fed on the milk of God's Word to enhance our spiritual growth and development.

With this in mind, first Corinthians 3:1-2 reads; *"And I, brethren, could not speak unto you as unto spiritual, but as unto carnal, even as unto babes in Christ. I have fed you with milk, and not with meat: for hitherto ye were not able to bear it, neither yet now are ye able."* Unfortunately, most people at no time go past this dimension of God's Word, moving on to the more advanced Christian teachings that will engender their spiritual development, thereby causing Spiritual malnutrition and never coming to a place of maturity where they can rely on God's Word as their guarantee.

Meat Dimension of God's Word: As aforementioned in 1 Corinthians 3:1-2, it is imperative that we grow to spiritual maturity by feeding on the meat of the Word of God. The Greek word for *"meat"* comes from the Greek word *Brōma* (Strong's G1033) meaning the more solid, complete and more profound spiritual doctrines of the Scriptures.

Apostle Paul observed and elaborated that the Church in Corinth was unable to rightly apprehend and usefully apply more difficult parts of divine truths of God's Word because they were still at the milk dimension of the Word of God. This shows that there is no substitute for reading and attending to the meat of the Word of God on a consistent basis. To experience God's Word as the final arbiter in all matters of life, we must prayerfully spend time in the Word of God.

Strong Meat Dimension of God's Word: Hebrews 5:12 reads: *"For when for the time ye ought to be teachers, ye have need that one teach you again which be the first principles of the oracles of God; and are become such as have need of milk, and not of strong meat."* The Greek words translated as *strong meat* are *Stereós* (Strong's G4731) and *Trophé* (Strong's G5160) respectively, meaning strong, stable, or steadfast nourishment.

The idea here is that most believers are incapable of receiving the profound teachings of the Scriptures as much as children are unable to digest solid meat. Thus, if you must grow and mature in your ability to deal with the affairs of life, it is imperative that you learn to handle the Word of God effectively. Therefore, you must engage and give yourself to the strong meat dimension of God's Word. As a result, you will experience God's Word as your ultimate guarantee.

Incorruptible Seed Dimension of God's Word: In First Peter 1:23, Apostle Peter writes: *"Being born again, not of corruptible seed, but of incorruptible, by the word of God, which liveth and abideth for ever."* Here the Greek word used for *"incorruptible"* is *Áphthartos* (Strong's G862), and it refers to something that is not liable to corruption or decay. Therefore, with great comfort and assurance in the fact that the incorruptible seed of God's Word is beyond any corruption, we must believe that God's Word is our ultimate guarantee.

The Word of God is often referred to as a seed. There are a total of forty-four verses in the New Testament where the Greek word *Spérma* (Strong's G4690) is translated *"seed."* We derive our English word "sperm" from this same word. The Word of God is the incorruptible seed that regenerates the hearer, bringing new life to those who receive it by faith. A seed is alive and viable, but a seed does nothing until it is planted in the soil to produce a mighty harvest; so also the seed of God's Word must be planted in our hearts to yield extraordinary results.

In the parable well elaborated in Mark 4:1-34, it is evident that Jesus is not trying to make a farmer out of you but to use natural things to illustrate spiritual truth. Consequently, when you are reading God's Word and letting it saturate you, change your attitude. Your experience and perception is the function of the seed of God's Word. The best way to plant the seed of God's Word in your life is to speak the Word, to hear others speak the Word, to study the Word, to meditate, and to memorize God's Word. Begin now, and as you do, you will start sowing the seed of God's Word into your life; you will experience God as your guarantee. The Word of God is the "seed" that brings new life (see Luke 8:11).

CHAPTER 3

IMPORTANCE OF GOD'S WORD

"And he said unto them, 'Set your hearts unto all the Words which I testify among you this day, which ye shall command your children to observe to do, all the words of this law. For it is not a vain thing for you; because it is your life: and through this thing, ye shall prolong your days in the land, whither ye go over Jordan to possess it" (Deuteronomy 32:46-47).

The significance of God's Word in every aspect of your human existence cannot be overemphasized. God's Word is the authentic source of power and wisdom. With this power and knowledge, you can reign over the works of darkness and live an extraordinary life that honors and glorifies God in your world. As the text above suggests, God's Word is not a vain thing for you, deserving of your undivided attention, in fact, the Word of God is not empty and meaningless words void of life and power, but the very essence of God. And indeed, your life depends on it. Consequently, your obedience to God's Words is what guarantees your place and the fulfilling of your days here on earth.

God's Word has the innate power to turn your life around, making you a wonder and a testament to your world.

Brother Job declares,

> *"Neither have I gone back from the commandment of his lips; I have esteemed the words of his mouth more than my necessary food"* (Job 23:12).

As far as Job was concerned, God's Word was much more important to him than his food, thus, indicating that God's Word cannot be substituted for your physical food. As natural food is required for the nourishment of your physical body to sustain life, likewise God's Word is necessary to nourish your human spirit to maintain the life of the Spirit. The Psalmist remarked, *"How sweet are thy words unto my taste! Yea, sweeter than honey to my mouth!"* (Psalms 119:103).

Jeremiah, on the other hand, had this to say, *"Thy words were found, and I did eat them; and thy word was unto me the joy and rejoicing of mine heart: for I am called by thy name, O Lord God of hosts"* (Jeremiah 15:16). God's Word imparts joy, causing the rejoicing of your hearts. It impregnates you with faith, courage, hope, and builds your love for Him and others.

God's Word is your life, your faith, your source of strength, and your anchor. We can put absolute confidence in the Word of God without wavering, knowing that He will bring to fruition that which He has spoken concerning you. It is, therefore, imperative that you study, meditate, and feed on the Word of God on a daily basis. God's Word brings tremendous transformation in the believers' lives.

The Lord Jesus Christ in His discourse said:

> *"It is the spirit that quickeneth; the flesh profiteth nothing: the words that I speak unto you, they are spirit, and they are life"* (John 6:63).

The text above is one of those verses in the Bible that is often undoubtedly misunderstood. The word "Spirit," in the preceding text, evidently does not refer to the third personality of the Godhead, The Holy Spirit, for He adds, "The words that I speak unto you, they are spirit." I believe that Jesus is referring to the doctrine that He had been teaching in opposition to their carnal views and desires that *"profiteth nothing,"* which add no value to man's deplorable condition of which he most needs redemption.

The Greek word for *"quickeneth"* is *Zōopoiéō* (Strong's G2227), a Greek compound word comprising *Zōon* (Strong's G2226), meaning "life" and *Poiéō* (Strong's G4160), meaning "to make." *Zōopoiéō* therefore denotes, to cause to live, to make alive, to give life, to invigorate or revitalize. This implies that the Word of God is spiritual and not to be understood literally. Furthermore, the spirit causes you to be alive or reinvigorated through God's Word, which is Spirit and Life.

It is important to know that living and experiencing the life of God entails receiving the Word of God, which is *Spirit* and *Life.* With that said, it's not enough to receive God's Word, but it must be acted upon in faith without wavering for it is when acted upon in faith that you can begin to experience the provisions and manifestation of God's Word in your life.

Hebrews 4:12 states, *"For the word of God is quick, and powerful, and sharper than any two-edged sword, piercing even to the dividing asunder of soul and spirit, and of the joints and marrow, and is a discerner of the thoughts and intents of the heart."* Here the Hebrew writer lets us know the potency of God's Word, as well as Apostle Paul who stresses that the Word of God is not merely a verbal message but a dynamic power that achieves things (see Acts 19:20). Thus, implying that the Word of God is unlike any other book you have in your home or in any additional place that is a mere collections of human ideas without the power to save.

The Scripture declares,

> *"Man shall not live by bread alone but by every word [Rhema] that proceedeth out of the mouth of God"* (Matthew 4: 4).

Here Jesus Christ alludes to the fact that you need food to live, but it is not exclusively sufficient in itself, as you also need the whole counsel of God's Word. God's *Rhema* commands and at the same time gives the believer strength to obey the command. It also equips the believer with power, and at the same time conveys faith for its fulfillment. It is, therefore, essential to understand that as you feed the natural body with natural food to survive, develop, and grow up physically, you should also feed on God's Word to survive, develop, and grow up spiritually. For as it is in the realm of the spirit, so it is in the realm of the natural. In essence, God's Word imparts life to you. It is a continual source of life for you (see Psalms 119:93).

You have to come to the understanding that God's Word is the absolute prerequisite for genuine spiritual growth, for the entrance of God's Word gives light, and it imparts knowledge and understanding to the simple (see Psalms 119:130). All your mental and spiritual insight and experiences will bring about lives devoid of the ability to reflect Christian maturity and genuine spiritual growth if separated from the application of God's Word (see James 1:21).

The Scripture teaches and admonishes us to:

> *"Let the word [spoken by] Christ (the Messiah) have its home [in your hearts and minds] and dwell in you in [all its] richness, as you teach and admonish and train one another in all insight and intelligence and wisdom [in spiritual things, and as you sing] psalms and hymns and spiritual songs, making melody to God with [His] grace in your hearts."* (Amplified Bible, Colossians 3:16).

Fundamentally, without God's Word, which is one of the most critical components needed for your walk of faith and spiritual maturity, you will be deceived about your progress, growth, and maturity in the things of God and your Christian walk of faith. Hence, Apostle Paul admonishes that if anyone thinks he is standing, he should be careful or else, he will stumble and fall (see 1 Corinthians 10:12). As you pursue intimacy with God, God's Word is an invaluable and indispensable resource.

> *"All scripture is given by inspiration of God and is profitable for doctrine, for reproof, for correction, for instruction in righteousness: That the man of God may be perfect, thoroughly furnished unto all good works"* (2 Timothy 3:16-17).

The word *"profitable"* in the preceding Scriptural text comes from the transliterated word *Ōphélimos* (Strong's G5624), which implies "useful, "profitable," "advantageous." That is, God's Word is useful, advantageous, and/or beneficial for teaching, for reproof, for correction, causing one to stand upright again and for instruction, which implies child rearing with discipline and chastening in righteousness. Consequently, we are to esteem no part of the Scripture as worthless. There is no portion of Scripture that may not be fitted, in certain circumstances, to provide us with valuable lessons. The result will be that the man of God is thoroughly furnished.

"Thoroughly furnished" expresses the intent of God. This word in Greek is *Exartízō* (Strong's G1822), and it is a compound word comprising *ek* (Strong's G1537) meaning *"out,"* and *Ártios* (Strong's G739), meaning *"complete, perfect." Exartízō*, therefore, denotes "to fit out," "to equip fully," "to complete," "to furnish perfectly," "to finish," "to accomplish." This implies that Scripture is sufficient for perfecting the man of God, thus, enhancing those qualifications that are necessary to complete the character and ensure the success of the man of God.

King David said,

> *"Thy word have I hid in mine heart, that I might not sin against thee"* (Psalms 119:11).

> *"I treasure your word above all else; it keeps me from sinning against you"* (Contemporary English Version).

This text must be adequately understood given that David had to consciously, deliberately, and voluntarily hide God's Word in his heart with the objective of not sinning against God. However, this is not the case among believers, but instead, all kinds of ridiculous activities such as using the Word for self-gratification have become so prevalent in Christendom today. God's Word in any man's heart will prevent him from going contrary to the commands of the Lord. Without God's Word in the human heart, they become vulnerable and an object of disgrace in the enemy's hand instead of becoming vessels of glory and honor unto God.

The Word of God hidden in your hearts is also essential because it helps you to live in harmony and good relations with one another. It helps you to see yourself in the light of Scriptures, thus helping you not to think more highly of yourself as the manner of some are. We tend to judge our performances in the light of worldly standards that fall short of Godly rules, and contrary to the dictates of God's Word. Apostle Paul warned:

> *"For I say, through the grace given unto me, to every man that is among you, not to think of himself more highly than he ought to think; but to think soberly, according as God hath dealt to every man the measure of faith"* (Romans 12:3).

Disobedience to the commands of God will separate you from God just like Adam and Eve experienced in the Garden of Eden when they disobeyed God's command (see Genesis 3). Once you heed Paul's admonition in the Scriptural text above, you will grow in God's Word, developing godly character and integrity. As you keep God's Word in your heart on a daily basis, it empowers you for an extraordinary life of victory over the works and the dictates of the flesh.

GOD'S WORD IS ETERNAL

. . . .

"The grass withereth, the flower fadeth: but the word of our God shall stand forever" (Isaiah 40: 8).

"Being born again, not of corruptible seed, but of incorruptible, by the word of God, which liveth and abideth for ever. For all flesh is as grass, and all the glory of man as the flower of grass. The grass withereth, and the flower thereof falleth away: But the word of the Lord endureth for ever. And this is the word which by the gospel is preached unto you" (1 Peter 1:23-25).

As insignificant as the grass and the flowers are, and as measureless as the heavens and the earth are, they will fade away and perish. In the text above, Apostle Peter draws a contrast between God's Word and man, elucidating that the Word of God endures forever while man is unstable in everything he does or produces just like flowers or grass that soon fades away and withers. Hence, trusting God's Word above all else is your ultimate guarantee.

God's Word does not have an origin of life neither does it have an end for it is never out of date or antiquated. God's Word abides eternally beyond any possibility of corruption. The Gospel of Matthew puts it plainly: *"Heaven and earth shall pass away, but my words shall not pass away,"* and the Psalmist declares, *"Forever, O Lord, thy word is settled in heaven"* (Matthew 24: 35; Psalms 119:89). God's Word cannot and will not lose its life-giving power, for God and His Word are eternally whole and inseparable. Apostle

John further elucidates that the word of God cannot be broken or disannulled (see John 10:35).

There has never been a time that God's Word did not exist, for God and His Word are eternally inseparable, meaning that as much as God is eternally immutable, so is His Word. Isaiah, the Prophet, spoke of God's Word as eternal (see Isaiah 40:8). The Word of God is more authoritative than your prevailing circumstances, and as you put your confidence in the eternal counsel of God's Word, victory on all fronts will be possible.

The Lord exhorted through the Prophet Isaiah:

> *"For as the rain cometh down, and the snow from heaven, and returneth not thither, but watereth the earth, and maketh it bring forth and bud, that it may give seed to the sower, and bread to the eater: So shall my word be that goeth forth out of my mouth: it shall not return unto me void, but it shall accomplish that which I please, and it shall prosper in the thing whereto I sent it"* (Isaiah 55:10-11).

God's mind and counsel revealed through His Word will stand unaltered and unadulterated now and through eternity" (see Matthew 24:35). The Word of God is His will. It is eternally valid and never fails in its plans and purposes. This conveys the perspective of the ageless, timeless, dateless, and infinite nature of God and His Word. Consequently, His Word that has gone out of His mouth concerning your life will have immediate and eternal consequence over your life. You can rest assured that you can rely on God and His Word as your ultimate guarantee.

GOD'S WORD SANCTIFIES

. . . .

> *"Now ye are clean through the word which I have spoken unto you"* (John 15:3).

"Sanctify them through thy truth: thy word is truth"
(John 17:17).

"That he might sanctify and cleanse it with the washing of water by the word" (Ephesians 5: 26).

The above Scriptural texts point out the means of sanctification and the importance of God's Word in the process. God's Word is a reliable and an undisputable medium in progressively bringing the believer to increase more and more in grace and holiness. According to Webster's Revised Unabridged Dictionary 1913,

To "sanctify" implies

1. To make sacred or holy; to set apart to a holy or religious use; to consecrate by appropriate rites; to hallow.
2. To make free from sin; to cleanse from moral corruption and pollution; to purify.
3. To make efficient as the means of holiness; to render productive of holiness or piety.
4. To impart or impute sacredness, venerableness, inviolability, title to reverence and respect, or the like, to secure from the violation; to give sanction to.

The Biblical context implies God setting apart the believer for Himself or His service. The word *"sanctify"* in the Greek is *Hagiazo* (Strong's G37), which means, *"to hallow or make holy," "to set apart," "to dedicate," "to consecrate" or "to be separate"* especially for holy use. The only way the Word of God can be a cleansing agent in our lives is when we hear, study, memorize, and meditate God's Word, allowing the Word to work in our lives through submission and obedience.

The Word of God makes you holy and sets you apart from the world unto God's purpose and plans. The Scripture declares, *"Now ye are clean through the word which I have spoken unto you"* (John 15:3). The Greek word for *"clean"* is *katharós* (Strong's G2513), meaning "to be free from the pollution and the guilt of sin, free from impure admixtures, spotless and without blemish." God's Word is potent enough to cleanse us of impure desires and unholy dispositions as we study, receive and meditate upon it on a consistent basis.

Apostle Paul exhorts you to allow the Word of Christ to dwell richly in your hearts (see Colossians 3:16). The more God's Word resides in your heart, the more you are purified and susceptible to the workings of the Word. As believers, we are often inundated with so many impure thoughts and unholy stuff throughout the day as we go about our daily activities, and if these unholy dispositions are unchecked, untold damage and setbacks will follow, and it will impede and affect our walk of faith. Therefore, it is imperative to allow God's Word to dwell in you richly, dominating and cleaning your heart daily.

The believer must, in the words of Luke 6:45, understand that a good man out of the good treasures of his heart, his mouth speaks. The word "*good*" in Greek is *Agathós* (Strong's G18), meaning good things, benefits, while the word "*treasure*" in Greek is *Thesaurós* (Strong's G2344), meaning wealthy deposits. Therefore, good treasure implies wealthy deposits in the heart of man that, when spoken, brings benefits to the speaker and those around him. Consequently, if the heart is not cleansed and dominated by God's Word but instead filled with unworthy deposits, whatever proceeds out of your mouth will be contrary to the Word of God and His intents for your life. To speak God's Word, you must allow the Word of God to dwell in your heart richly and in abundance.

GOD'S WORD ACTS LIKE
FIRE AND HAMMER

. . . .

"'Is not my word like as a fire?' saith the Lord; 'and like a hammer that breaketh the rock in pieces?'" (Jeremiah 23:29).

The prophet Jeremiah helps us understand by the Spirit of God that the Word of God acts like fire and a hammer. What is it that the Holy Spirit wants us to understand by using *fire* and *hammer* as metaphors to describe God's Word? Well, we know that one of the attributes of fire is that it serves as a purifier. Consequently, God's Word acting like fire helps to get rid of the impurities in our hearts and minds through the process of burning up every chaff or trace of the flesh (impurities) in our lives.

Apostle Paul admonishes us in Romans 12:2, *"And be not conformed to this world: but be ye transformed by the renewing of your mind, that ye may prove what is the good, and acceptable, and perfect, will of God."* It is essential to understand that to be *transformed* here is not just a change in one aspect of life but a total turnaround. The Greek word used is *Metamorphóo* (Strong's G3339), where we obtain the English word *metamorphosis*, meaning complete change from one state of existence to another: a total turnaround. This transformation occurs in your life when you study, take heed, and make God's Word your final authority.

Like a hammer, God's Word serves to disintegrate everything that is unclean in the heart of man and bring about conviction. Acts 2:37 says, *"When they heard this, they were pricked in their heart, and said unto Peter and to the rest of the apostles, 'Men and brethren, what shall we do?'"* The Word of God can produce conviction of sin in the heart of man that can lead to repentance and as a result, create a heart of flesh in him.

> *"For the Word of God is quick, and powerful, and sharper than any two-edged sword, piercing even to the dividing asunder of soul and spirit, and of the joints and marrow, and is a discerner of the thoughts and intents of the heart"* (Hebrews 4:12).

In the text above, the Greek word for *"quick"* is Záo (Strong's G2198), meaning *"to be in full vigor,"* *"to live,"* *"to be powerful."* The power of the Word of God can transform your life if you allow it to do its work in the innermost parts of your heart and mind. It will, like fire, burn any traces of impurity and like a hammer remove unclean thoughts and desires that are contrary to the thoughts and ways of God. In John 6:63, Jesus said, *"It is the spirit that quickeneth; the flesh profiteth nothing: the words that I speak unto you, they are spirit, and they are life.*

God's Word has life, and it carries God's DNA code to create and reproduce after the intents of God's heart. In Luke 8, Jesus likened the Word of God to a seed. We all know that a seed has life and the potential to create after its kind.

Your heart was made for God's Word. God created His Word to be placed in your heart. The Word of God has life and the potential to grow when planted in the fertile soil of your heart. As it grows, it produces fruits of righteousness, renews your mind, changes the way things work in your life, and causes them to align with the will and plans of God for your life.

GOD'S WORD IS CREATIVE

. . . .

"By the word of the LORD were the heavens made; and all the host of them by the breath of his mouth" (Psalms 33:6).

"For this they willingly are ignorant of, that by the word of God the heavens were of old, and the earth standing out of the water and in the water" (2 Peter 3:5).

As you release the Word of God out of your mouth over your situations, you are releasing the creative ability of God into that circumstance. Most of the time, it is easier for a believer to doubt in moments of trials and difficulties because of their ignorance of the creative power of the Word of God. Irrespective of what you may be experiencing, I encourage you to release the Word of God, and as you do so, you will be unleashing the creative power of God's Word in that situation, and you will begin to see and experience the hand of God working in and through your life.

God's Word Restrains from Evil

· ·

"Concerning the works of men, by the word of thy lips I have kept me from the paths of the destroyer" (Psalms 17:4).

"Thy word have I hid in mine heart, that I might not sin against thee" (Psalms 119:11).

The Psalmist declares in the above text that God's Word kept him from the part of the destroyer. The word *"kept"* in this verse is *Shâmar* (Strong's H8104), which means: "to guard," "to hedge about," "to protect," and "to attend to." The Word of God has inherent power to protect you from the destroyer and its attacks. Anyone void of God's Word is susceptible to all kinds of satanic harassment. Hence, holding onto God's Word as your guarantee is beyond measure. Take heed, therefore, to Psalms 119:11, the Psalmist's warning, which states that we should protect the Word of God in our hearts so as not to go contrary to the ways of God. It is of utmost importance that you understand that none of the schemes of the enemy against you, your family and your enterprise, will come nigh you.

God's Word Heals

· ·

"He sent his word, and healed them, and delivered them from their destructions" (Psalms 107:20).

This is a remarkable statement, yet it is true, and millions of men have been healed and delivered by the power of God's Word.

29

We also discover from the creation account that the Word of God is powerful and efficient (see Genesis 1:3). God's Word has inherent healing power; it can deliver you from oppression and all that endangers your life.

Consider Proverbs 4:20-22 which says, *"My son, attend to my words; incline thine ear unto my sayings. Let them not depart from thine eyes; keep them in the midst of thine heart. For they are life unto those that find them, and health to all their flesh."* There are life and health in God's Word. Thank God for medical intervention. However, man is not healed by human medications alone, but by the incorruptible Word that proceeds out of the mouth of God.

He has sent His Word; it has already gone forth so you can be confident that healing and deliverance are already yours, only start confessing and standing on God's Word by faith for your healing miracle in the name of Jesus and you have what you confess. God's Word is God's will, and so, when we pray God's Will for our lives, we are praying His Word to heal our bodies, situations, and all things by His Word.

The centurion understood the power of the Word and as a result, demanded that Jesus did not need to come to his house but requested that He speak the Word only, and his servant would be healed. The Lord Jesus responded by speaking and sending the Word, and the centurion's servant was healed from that very hour in which the Word was spoken (see Matthew 8:7-8). The Word of God is active and powerful: distance is not a barrier to its efficacy. God sends a Word and releases a power on earth that ultimately remedies whatever problem it is addressed to.

GOD'S WORD HAS THE POWER TO SAVE

. . . .

"Wherefore lay apart all filthiness and superfluity of naughtiness, and receive with meekness the engrafted word, which is able to save your souls" (James 1:21).

"And that from a child thou hast known the holy scriptures, which are able to make thee wise unto salvation through faith which is in Christ Jesus" (2 Timothy 3:15).

The Greek word for *"save"* in the Scriptural text above is *Sōzō* (Strong's G4982), which means "to save, keep safe and sound, to rescue from danger or destruction." God's Word has inherent power to keep us unharmed, liberating us from the onslaught of the enemy. No matter the enemy's weapon of mass destruction, the Word of God is much more than enough to paralyze, render impotent, and frustrate the enemy's onslaught.

To experience the unstoppable power of God's Word in our lives, James tells us that there are things that we must lay aside. In James 1:21a, He mentions such things as "superfluity of naughtiness" or as rendered by the NKJV "all filthiness and overflow of wickedness." Above all else, we must endeavor to seek the kingdom of God and His righteousness.

GOD'S WORD IS AN UNERRING GUIDE

. . . .

"Thy word is a lamp to my feet, and a light to my path" (Psalms 119:105).

The above Scripture demonstrates and shows the importance of God's Word as our guide in all matters of life. God's Word acts as a lamp and is ever needful because man needs a guide through life, as the road is sometimes intricate and dark. We are often confronted with moments of uncertainty in our personal and professional lives, not knowing what to do. The Word of God throws light and illuminates every conceivable step in life, and the light is bright and sufficient. Those who hold God's Word before them will not stumble as they depend on the Word of God as their reliable guide.

CHAPTER 4

WHAT IS FAITH?

FAITH DEFINED

. . . .

"Now faith is the substance of things hoped for, the evidence of things not seen" (Hebrews 11: 1).

"Faith shows the reality of what we hope for; it is the evidence of things we cannot see" (New Living Translation, Hebrews 11:1).

"What is faith? It is the confident assurance that something we want is going to happen. It is the certainty that what we hope for is waiting for us, even though we cannot see it up ahead" (The Living Bible, Hebrews 11:1).

"Now faith is the assurance of things hoped for, the conviction of things not seen" (New American Standard, Hebrews 11:1).

"Now faith is confidence in what we hope for and assurance about what we do not see" (New International Version, Hebrews 11:1).

"Now faith is the assurance (the confirmation, the title deed) of the things [we] hope for, being the proof of things [we] do not see and the conviction of their reality [faith perceiving as real fact what is not revealed to the senses]" (Amplified Bible, Classic Edition Hebrews 11:1).

What is faith? It is that which gives substance to our hopes, which convinces us of things we cannot see (Knox Bible, Hebrews 11:1).

Faith is of the utmost importance, so we must understand what it is. Faith is believing and acting on God's Word. Without faith, no man can please God or gain anything from Him (see Hebrews 11:6). Everything about the kingdom of God primarily is accessed by faith and is kept by faith.

Webster's Dictionary 1828 defines faith saying, "The faith of the gospel is that emotion of the mind, which is called trust or confidence, exercised towards the moral character of God, and particularly of the Saviour. Faith is affectionate practical confidence in the testimony of God. Faith is a firm, cordial belief in the veracity of God, in all the declarations of his word; or full and affectionate confidence in the certainty of those things which God has declared, and because he has declared them."

The Greek word *Pístis* (Strong's G4102) is translated many times as "faith" in the Scriptures, which means a conviction or firm persuasion, trust, assurance, or confidence in another's word. Another interesting Greek word for *"faith"* is *Pisteuó* (Strong's G4100), and this noun corresponds to the verb *"to believe, entrust."* This is the term used most often to denote trust in God. Therefore, faith in God is simply trusting and being obedient to God.

Faith is that unwavering confidence in God, which is built upon absolute trust in His integrity, believing and acting upon His Word. Scriptural faith is the unshaken confidence that what God says in His Word is so even though at present there is no other evidence that it is so. It is having assurance in Him that His Word is valid and that He is faithful in His promises, keeping and performing His Word. Conclusively, we can infer that faith is merely a response to God's Word, a deep conviction, and belief that His Words are true and that He is able to fulfill His promises.

EPIGRAM ON FAITH

- Faith is not a philosophical fact; neither is it an intellectual fact; faith is a spiritual force, drawn from the living word to produce living proofs (**Bishop David Oyedepo**).
- Faith-filled words (flowing from our hearts) give us victory; fear-filled words defeat us (**Dr. Norvel Hayes**).
- We will walk in the level of life where we release the ability of God by the words of our mouth (**Marilyn Hickey**).
- Your tongue is the most powerful weapon and force of your life (**Kenneth Hagin**).
- You will never realize anything beyond the words you speak (**Dr. Don Gossett**).
- Faith sees the invisible, believes the incredible, and receives the impossible (**David Lloyd George**).
- Faith is to accept the impossible, do without the indispensable, and bear the intolerable (**David Lloyd George**).
- Faith is idle when circumstances are right, only when they are adverse is one's faith in God exercised. Faith, like a muscle, grows strong and supple with exercise (**David Lloyd George**).
- Don't be afraid to take a big step if one is indicated. You can't cross a chasm in two small jumps (**David Lloyd George**).

- A little faith will bring your soul to heaven; a great faith will bring heaven to your soul (**Charles Haddon Spurgeon**).
- Faith is not believing that God can, but that God will! (**Abraham Lincoln**).
- Faith is to believe what we do not see, and the reward of this faith is to see what we believe (**Saint Augustine**).
- Faith is seeing the invisible, but not the nonexistent (**A.W. Tozer**).

Faith is not a bare belief or intellectual understanding of God's Word but a firm conviction, resting on God's Word that makes the future present and the invisible seen. It is a willingness to trust in, to rely on, and to cling to the Word of God regardless of life's drama. It is also an essential channel through which man receives God's gift of salvation and appropriate covenant promises in his life.

Faith is also a covenant relationship based on belief in the faithfulness and ability of God to do that which His Word declares He will do (see Isaiah 55:10-11). The Scriptures let us understand in Ephesians 2:8 that *"For by grace are ye saved through faith; and that not of yourselves: it is the gift of God."* Thank God, for the gracious gift of salvation bestowed upon us. However, it is through the instrumentality of faith that we can receive and appropriate this gift.

The eleventh chapter of Hebrews is the famous chapter on faith. The first verse is not just an introduction to faith or its definition, but also a description of what faith does. Faith apprehends as fact what is not revealed or accessible to the senses. It rests on that fact, acts upon it, and is upheld by it in the face of all that seems to contradict it. The understanding of Hebrews 11:1 is that faith considers things hoped for as authentic and as the proof or conviction of what you do not see or that, which cannot be perceived by your natural senses.

Faith is not based on the evidence of your physical senses but the realities revealed by God's Word (see 2 Corinthians 5:7). You do not base your faith on that which is seen or experienced in the natural. Therefore, faith is not a persuasion that is the outcome of the imagination but that, which is based on the integrity of God's Word.

Let us examine the following words *"substance"* and *"evidence"* in Hebrews 11:1. The Greek word for *"substance"* is *Hypóstasis* (Strong's G5287), and it is made up of two compound words *Hypó* (Strong's G5259), meaning "under," and *Hístēmi* (Strong's G2476), meaning "hold up," to stand firm." Therefore, *Hypóstasis* implies that *"which underlines the apparent, essence or reality, support, groundwork, confidence, confirmation, title deed, that which is the basis of something, that which becomes a foundation for another thing to stand on."*

Additionally, Thayer's Greek Lexicon defines *Hypóstasis* as *"a setting or placing under; thing put under, substructure, foundation: that which has foundation, is firm; hence, that which has actual existence; a substance, real being."* Faith, therefore, is that which holds up, that which you are hoping for but have not yet seen.

On the other hand, the Greek word for *"evidence"* is *Élenchos* (Strong's G1650). It is a legal term meaning "evidence that is accepted for conviction, proof, that by which a thing is proved or tested, conviction or persuasion of things not seen, demonstration or manifestation." Therefore, *Élenchos* implies *"that by which we readily perceive or apprehend what we do not see based on the God's Word producing something that furnishes proof."*

Furthermore, Thayer's Greek Lexicon defines it as that by which invisible things are proved or tested, and we are persuaded of their reality. Just as your physical eyesight is the sense that gives you evidence of the material world, so also faith is the sense that gives you evidence of the invisible, the things you hope for but not yet seen. Our faith is the proof, conviction, or persuasion of what we are hoping for or believing God will do and that we have received what we hope for even when it is not physically visible.

Apostle Paul further emphasizes in 2 Corinthians 4: 18 NKJV that *"While we do not look at the things which are seen, but at the things which are not seen. For the things which are seen are temporary; but the things which are not seen are eternal."* Your human senses deal with things that are temporal and changeable, but faith deals with things that are invisible, eternal, and unchanging, which is unperceivable to man's physical senses.

The phrase *"things hoped for"* comes from the Greek word *Elpizó* (Strong's G1679), which means to hope, to have a favorable and confident expectation. Things hoped for always exist beyond the realm of visibility, that which cannot be seen or perceived with the natural senses. However, its non-visibility is not an indication of its non-existence. This suggests that things hoped for, yet not seen or experienced in the physical, exist in the supernatural and have higher tangibility than the things seen or experienced in the material world.

The substance (essence or reality, title deed, support or ground work), the evidence (proof, that by which a thing is proved or tested or conviction) of things hoped for and yet not seen is *faith*. Scriptural faith treats things hoped for as real, the proof or manifestation of what is unseen as being real. In reality, for faith to be activated, it is necessary to hope for things. This suffices to say that a lack of things hoped for could be one of the reasons why many believers are not experiencing the potency of faith and its demonstration in their lives. Hence, most believers are swift to conclude that the message of faith is beside the point and impotent. This is an unscriptural and erroneous conclusion. Faith goes to work and becomes operative where there are things hoped for and yet not seen in the natural realm.

Considering faith as the manufacturer and hope as the raw material that is the primary material from which a product is created will bring clarity to the confusion that has persisted for such a long time and has robbed many of their spiritual breakthroughs in life. It is reasonable to infer that without the raw material, the manufacturer will have nothing to work on or work with to produce the desired product. This is true of faith, for, without hope, faith has nothing to work on or with to create the desired result in our lives as it were.

THE SOURCE OF FAITH

. . . .

"How then shall they call on him in whom they have not believed? and how shall they believe in him of whom they have not heard? and how shall they hear without a preacher? And how shall they preach, except they be sent? as it is written, 'How beautiful are the feet of them that preach the gospel of peace, and bring glad tidings of good things!' But they have not all obeyed the gospel. For Esaias saith, 'Lord, who hath believed our report? So then faith cometh by hearing and hearing by the word of God'" (Romans 10: 14-17).

"Howbeit many of them which heard the word believed; and the number of the men was about five thousand" (Acts 4:4).

The Word of God is the instrument God has appointed for us and that which He uses to impart faith. In the above text, Apostle Paul lets us understand that faith comes as a result of God's Word being heard; it is, therefore, appropriate to infer that faith has its source in the Word of God. Faith is developed and strengthened by the Word of God heard and received. This is the kind of faith we need to demonstrate referenced by Jesus in Mark 11:22-23 when He says that you can move mountains if only you believe and do not doubt. In Acts 4:4, it is stated that many heard the Word of God and believed. This also indicates that faith comes from hearing God's Word preached.

Jesus Christ is the living Word, and the Bible is the written Word of God. The written Word must be quickened into your heart to produce Scriptural faith. Faith is linked to God's Word; it comes by hearing and hearing by the Word of God. This shows us at once the importance of the Word and the fact that faith is produced in men by the instrumentality of God's Word.

If faith is not built upon God's Word, it cannot resist the storms and tests of life. Faith once produced must be based on and sustained by God's Word to bring about the desired results. The more you hear the Word of God, the more your faith increases. Contrary to popular notion, it's of utmost importance to understand that it's impossible to separate God's Word from faith and vice-versa.

The Apostle Paul in Romans 12:3 elucidates that God has given to everyone "the *measure of faith.*" The Greek word for *"measure"* is *Métron* (Strong's G3358). It means "a measure, an instrument for measuring," "a vessel for receiving and determining the quantity of things whether dry or liquid," "proverbially, the rule or standard of judgment," a measure of capacity. In the context of the above verse, Apostle Paul speaks of the measure of capacity as his reference, implying that we can function in life by the measure of faith apportioned to us.

However, for the panoramic view of our study, "measure of faith" implies that God has allotted to the believer a level, volume, or quantity of faith that can increase or be developed as an athlete develops his or her muscles. The Bible says, *"So mightily grew the word of God and prevailed"* (Acts 19:20) and *"But the word of God grew and multiplied"* (Acts 12:24). These two verses of Scriptures teach us that God's Word has a propensity to grow and increase. In the same way, faith can grow and increase, since its source is God's Word.

Consequently, it is imperative to know that whatever you do or don't do with that measure of faith you have received is solely your responsibility and prerogative. This, of course, is relevant to how the measure of faith that you have received increases or decreases. To increase the measure of faith, you must feed on the Word of God and exercise it, for faith without corresponding action is dead (see James 2:17). According to Hebrews 5:12-14, a mature believer is a person who ought to put the Word into practice.

Faith comes by *hearing* and *hearing* comes by the *Word of God.* The Word of God studied, spoken, or heard and quickened into your spirit produces faith. Understanding God's Word will not just create faith, but it will begin a process in your heart; therefore, the consistent hearing of God's Word builds and increases faith, which doubtlessly becomes *the substance* of things hoped for, *the evidence* of things not seen.

If faith comes by hearing, then you should make it a habit to speak and pray the Word of God daily, this will help to increase your faith. Do not go around saying what you think is right, or how you feel about your circumstances; it will be more profitable and rewarding when you say what God's Word declares as it is the final arbiter for your life. After all, what He says is complete truth for God is not a man that He should lie (see Numbers 23:19).

Furthermore, the Scripture declares, *"without faith, it is impossible to please God"* Hebrews 11:6, thus implying that pleasing God depends on living and walking by faith. If faith is necessary to please God and it is a product of God's Word, to please God, therefore, is to operate within the confines of His Word, which means that pleasing God is predicated on obeying God and His Word. Faith thus is the primary component needed to activate God's Word to produce desired results such as healings, deliverances, and God's Word must equally be the fundamental component on which faith is built to become useful in its workings.

If the arm of flesh produces faith, it has to depend on and be sustained by it. This has caused disappointment for many sincere Christians, who, out of ignorance of God's Word, have based their faith on the arm of flesh instead of basing it on God's Word. The arm of flesh signifies human strength or help, thus to trust in the arm of flesh is to believe in the human wisdom and effort to achieve that which only God can bring to fruition through "the Word of His power" (see Hebrews 1:3).

The Scripture declares: *"Thus saith the Lord; 'Cursed be the man that trusteth in man, and maketh flesh his arm, and whose heart departeth from the Lord'"* (Jeremiah 17:5). Here, the Scripture emphatically stresses that the man or woman who makes the flesh his or her confidence is one whose heart has departed from the Lord, the consequence thereof being a curse.

When faith is at work, the power of God is at work, which makes the impossible possible. Faith is your access to God's power.

Without faith, nothing is completed; and without faith, God cannot be pleased (see Hebrews 11:6).

God's Word produces faith and faith = the substance of things hoped for, the evidence of things not seen.

Consequently, God's Word = faith = the substance of things hoped for, the evidence of things not seen.

Considering the above equation, it is true that God's Word becomes the substance of things hoped for and the evidence of things not seen. It is imperative to understand that the things hoped for are the same as the things not yet seen, for this is what the Spirit of the Lord implies through Apostle Paul in (Romans 8:24) when he declares, *"For we are saved by hope: but hope that is seen is not hope: for what a man seeth, why doth he yet hope for?"* That is, if you are hoping for healing and have experienced healing, why yet hope for the healing you already possess. It is no longer hope because it has already manifested.

Conclusively, God's Word is the *substance* of things hoped for, the *evidence* of things not seen. In other words, the Word of God that you have received with your heart becomes the substance (essence, support or title deed), the evidence (proof or conviction) that in spite of your present realities, you have what you are hoping for but yet not seen in the physical. God's Word gives substance and validity to the immaterial.

In effect, in the time between the expectation of things hoped for that are yet to be seen, and the physical manifestation of those things, God's Word is your guarantee, the substance and the evidence that you possess those things for which you believe God. Understand that God is not a man that He should lie. If He said it, He *will* perform, perfect, and bring it to fruition. God is faithful to His Word, and we can experience the promises of His Word when we rely on and put our complete and unequivocal dependence on God's Word.

If healing, for instance, is the *thing hoped for*, the *thing not seen*, faith, therefore, is the substance, the evidence that occurs as a result of God's Word received through hearing, study, and meditation. You must believe that you are already healed, regardless of what the symptoms indicate in the natural. When standing on God's Word for your healing and the signs of the illness are still physically evident, the symptoms should not determine your condition, but God's Word received, which is the substance and evidence of the healing until there is a physical manifestation of what you are hoping and for which you are trusting God.

For instance (Hebrews 11:11) declares,

> *"Through faith also Sarah herself received strength to conceive seed, and was delivered of a child when she was past age, because she judged him faithful who had promised."*

Sarah received God's Word in the midst of impossibility and uncertainty, but she held on, trusting God's Word, while that Word was working mightily on her behalf. She made up her mind to receive her miracle irrespective of the mountain of impossibilities, thus, consciously judging God faithful that what He had promised He was able to accomplish. What this meant to her was that it was undoubtedly done and God's Word was the final arbiter of her situation. Moreover, God is not a respecter of persons (see Acts 10:34) as He did for Sarah, He will do for you much more if only you believe His Word as your ultimate guarantee.

The Greek word translated *"respecter"* is *Prosōpolḗptēs* (Strong's G3358). It means, to show favoritism, one exhibiting partiality, one who discriminates. In contrast, that God is no respecter of persons implies that He is impartial, He is not biased in His dealings with His creation. Therefore, what He does for one He will do for the other. He will do for you only if you believe that He can do exceedingly above what you think or imagine.

KNOWLEDGE BORN OF FAITH

. . . .

> *"Through faith we understand that the worlds were framed by the word of God, so that things which*

are seen were not made of things which do appear"
(Hebrews 11:3).

The Bible reliably asserts that no one can receive its message and experience its dynamics without faith. In the text above, I want you to see that the principle of *knowledge* imparted by *faith* is applied to the story of creation, but this principle is equally applicable to all parts of the Bible. The Bible in Basic English version (BBE) renders the text above thus: *"By faith it is clear to us that the order of events was fixed by the word of God, so that what is seen has not been made from things which only seem to be."* What is the principle demonstrated here? It is simply: *"by faith we know."* Knowledge is born by faith. Ipso facto, faith must come through the knowledge of God's Word (see Proverbs 18:15).

There is a kind of knowledge or comprehension that only faith can produce and in no other way can this kind of knowledge be accessible. As we progress through life, we imbibe a lot of information because of our family orientation, education, experiences, and associations. However, there is a dimension of life or existence that God has ordained for His Children that mental knowledge acquired through the various means stated can never bring you. For instance, to solve our massive relationship problems and other insoluble dilemmas that overwhelm us. Only knowledge gained through faith in God's Word will be able to help us gain access to the life of God.

The Bible declares,

> *"But the natural man receiveth, not the things of the Spirit of God: for they are foolishness unto him: neither can he know them, because they are spiritually discerned"* (1 Corinthians 2:14).

Apostle Paul in the text mentioned above indicates that the natural man accepts evidence based on interpretation by human reasoning or what can be verified and validated by experiences but remains unresponsive to the Word of God. If you must live the life that God has ordained for you, you must apply the principle of *"by faith we know,"* which is why you are admonished to *"walk by faith and not by sight"* (2 Corinthians 5:7).

Therefore, irrespective of your circumstances or what the world throws at you, you must refrain from assessing situations by carnal means. Faith brings its evidence, conveys its witness, and unlocks its understanding of God's Word, which ultimately produces God-kind-of-life in us. As you allow God's Word to permeate you, it will become your guarantee.

CHAPTER 5

HOW TO EXHIBIT YOUR FAITH

"For the which cause I also suffer these things: nevertheless I am not ashamed: for I know whom I have believed, and am persuaded that he is able to keep that which I have committed unto him against that day" (2 Timothy 1:12).

As believers, we tend to exhibit our faith in four significant ways: that is, believing, professing or confessing, sharing our faith or propagating, and contending or fighting for our faith. I dare to say that contending is one of the ways that most believers scarcely demonstrate their faith. In reality, the average believer believes, professes, and shares his or her belief with almost no thought of contending for it. As a result of this, we tend to compromise in so many areas concerning the faith that we believe, profess, and propagate.

It is of the utmost importance to have the understanding that for our faith to be efficacious, we must engage these four processes.

To Believe

"For verily I say unto you, 'That whosoever shall say unto this mountain, "Be thou removed, and be thou cast into the sea"; and shall not doubt in his heart, but shall believe that those things which he saith shall come to pass; he shall have whatsoever he saith"' (Mark 11:23).

"I promise you, if anyone says to this mountain, Remove, and be cast into the sea, and has no hesitation in his heart, but is sure that what he says is to come about, his wish will be granted him" (Know Bible, Mark 11:23).

"Jesus said unto him, 'If thou canst believe, all things are possible to him that believeth'" (Mark 9:23).

The Greek word for *"believe"* is *Pisteúō* (Strong's G4100), which means to have faith (in, upon, or concerning a person or thing), to trust, to place full confidence in, to rest upon with faith. Merely put, believing is faith with the corresponding action. Therefore, to believe in God is to rely upon, or put confidence in God Himself. When you believe God, you trust His Word; when you believe in God, you trust God (Himself). When you believe God, you do not stagger, but you fix your eyes on what He has said in His Word (see Romans 4:20-21). When you believe in God, you set your sight upon what He is, upon His person.

As a matter of fact, in Mark 11:14, Jesus with His twelve disciples were leaving Bethany, Jesus was hungry and seeing a fig tree from afar, He went to find out if it had any fruit to eat. On getting there, He discovered there was nothing edible except leaves because it was not the season for figs. Consequently, Jesus spoke to the fig tree that, "No man eat fruit of thee hereafter forever. And the disciples heard it" (see Mark 11:11-14).

The next day as they passed by, the disciples were much astonished at the outcome of Jesus' declaration over the fig tree the previous night. Peter focused his attention on it, while Jesus responded to their incomprehension, saying that whatever they proclaimed without doubting in their heart but believed, not only would they see mountains removed and cast into the sea, but they would also experience the kind of outcome they had just witnessed with their very own eyes. Consequently, for your faith to be productive and for God's Word to become the final arbiter of your life, I strongly encourage you to believe in God, act upon His Word, and declare it aloud daily.

Profession/Confession of Your Faith

"Seeing then that we have a great high priest, that is passed into the heavens, Jesus the Son of God, let us hold fast our profession" (Hebrews 4:14).

"Let us hold fast the profession of our faith without wavering; (for he is faithful that promised;)" (Hebrews 10:23).

Hebrews 4:14 and 10:23, respectively, let us understand the importance of holding fast the confession of our faith in Him. The Greek word for *"profession" or "confession"* in this text is *Homología* (Strong's G3671), which implies to speak the same thing, to profess or acknowledge openly, to express the same thing, to assent, accord, agree with, declare, and admit. What does the Scripture mean when it says that you should hold on to the profession of your faith? It signifies that we should hold fast to our confession, as we would hold fast to something that someone or something was trying to take away from us.

Indeed, the enemy and circumstances will try to steal or adulterate our confession. Therefore, we should not allow this to happen. How do I do just that in the midst of imminent danger? We do just that by focusing on and confessing God's Word in spite of the condition. We must say the same thing that God has said about us in His Word and publicly acknowledge our faith.

Professing or confessing faith is another significant way through which believers exhibit their faith in God and His Word. This, in turn, empowers them and validates their faith-walk. You must have heard statements like, "I am not a professing Christian." That is ridiculous; there is nothing like a non-professing Christian. The bottom line is either you are a professing Christian or not a Christian at all.

Sharing Your Faith

> *"Go ye therefore, and teach all nations, baptizing them in the name of the Father, and of the Son, and of the Holy Ghost: Teaching them to observe all things whatsoever I have commanded you: and, lo, I am with you always, even unto the end of the world. Amen"* (Matthew 28:19-20).

Many Christians are intimidated by the idea of sharing their faith. Jesus never intended for the Great Commission to be an impossible burden. To propagate here, merely implies the sharing of your faith and telling others about Jesus Christ, the price He paid for your redemption and what He continues to do in your life. In sharing your faith, you become instrumental for the furtherance of God's purposes in every part of the world. Propagation of your faith is the response to what is referred to as the Great Commission in the Bible (see Matthew 28:19-20).

Our Savior and Lord Jesus Christ expects us to propagate our faith in the world because He told us so. Obedience to the Great Commission is another way that every believer ought to exhibit his or her faith in God, and it is a test of your love for the Master's cause. Apostle Paul writes in Romans 1:16, *"For I am not ashamed of the gospel of Christ: for it is the power of God unto salvation to every one that believeth; to the Jew first, and also to the Greek."* As believers, this also ought to be our attitude and profession of the gospel of our Lord and Savior, Jesus Christ.

Contending for the Faith

"Beloved, when I gave all diligence to write unto you of the common salvation, it was needful for me to write unto you, and exhort you that ye should earnestly contend for the faith which was once delivered unto the saints" (Jude 1:3).

"Fight the good fight of faith, lay hold on eternal life, whereunto thou art also called, and hast professed a good profession before many witnesses" (1Timothy 6:12).

Here, Jude admonishes us to earnestly contend for the faith, while Apostle Paul exhorts Timothy to fight the good fight of faith. Now in both instances, we understand that there is an enemy of our faith and that there is a raging battle to be fought and this battle is called the fight of faith.

The Greek word for *"earnestly contend"* is *Epagōnízomai* (Strong's G1864), which means to contend, to struggle for, to fight against, to wrestle, to refute or to reject. With this understanding, we should contend for our faith as a person fighting a war or battle; hence, we are not called to be passive in our faith walk but to be vigilant in the cause of Christ (see Philippians 1:27).

On the other hand, the Greek word for *"fight"* is *Agōnízomai* (Strong's G75), meaning "to struggle, to compete for a prize, to contend with an adversary, or to endeavor to accomplish something—fight, labor fervently, strive." The fight of faith is that fight that every Christian believer must be engaged in to gain mastery and enforce the victory that Jesus Christ procured for us at redemption.

My question to you today is: Is your Faith worth fighting for? As Apostle Paul admonishes young Timothy to fight the fight of faith (see 1 Timothy 6:12), likewise, it is imperative for us to understand that as believers, we are engaged in a fight. Indeed, there is an enemy to fight against, and there is something for which to fight.

Apostle Paul's admonition equally gives the impression that there is an enemy who always wages war against our faith with the intention of breaking our fellowship with God, hindering our spiritual progress, shipwrecking us, and rendering our service to the Lord useless and unfruitful. Therefore, according to 1 Timothy 6:12, Apostle Paul observes that this is a fight worth engaging in, for you to paralyze and render futile every onslaught of the enemy against you and the confession of your faith.

How to Contend for the Faith

One of the things most people often do not take into consideration is the fact that there is always a demand placed on knowledge acquired or possessed. Knowledge is not to be acquired for the sake of obtaining it, but it must be applied to get the benefit of the knowledge gained.

In the same light, you are often taught what you should do and shouldn't do with little or no instruction on how to do or not do it. As a result, most people are incapacitated in their pursuits. I will not only inform you about contending for the faith but will also give you instructions on how to do it so that you may be inspired and positioned to fight for the faith as you read this book.

Through God's Word

"And take the helmet of salvation, and the sword of the Spirit, which is the word of God." (Ephesians 6:17).

"'Is not my word like as a fire?' saith the Lord; and like a hammer that breaketh the rock in pieces?"
(Jeremiah 23:29)

God's Word is one of the mighty weapons in your arsenal, such as "the name of Jesus," "prayer," and "the blood of Jesus," just to cite a few that you can use to contend for the faith. As you consistently hear, receive, and feed on God's Word, your spirit is fed, nurtured, and armed with the sword that it wields in battle. As you must know, the enemy is going around seeking to destroy your faith (see 1 Peter 5:8).

It is with God's Word that you guard your faith against the enemy's attacks. Your knowledge and understanding of God's Word will help you negate all the lies and attacks of the devil. Apostle Peter teaches, *"As newborn babes"* you should *"desire the sincere milk"* of God's Word *"that you might grow thereby"* (1 Peter 2:2). As God's Word nourishes your spirits, it will begin to dwell in all its richness in your hearts, renewing your minds, thus, helping you to become strong, stable, active, and mature.

God's Word has inherent power and authority against demonic forces. It is the sword of the Spirit that enables you to engage and negate all the schemes of the enemy and live victoriously (see Luke 4:36). It can pull down the strongholds of Satan, and not only can you resist the devil's influence in your own lives, but you can also destroy the enemy's impact on the lives of others (2 Corinthians 10:4-5). Henceforth, no matter the onslaught with which the enemy assails you or the challenges that he confronts you with, you must contend with the Word of God to overcome and gain mastery in all areas of your life.

Through Prayers

"Praying always with all prayer and supplication in the Spirit, and watching thereunto with all perseverance and supplication for all saints;" (Ephesians 6:18).

This kind of prayer is Spirit-driven, energized, enabled, and directed. However, it is not limited to just praying in tongues but doing so alongside other forms of prayers initiated by the Holy Spirit's promptings, praying in the spirit and your understanding. Jude admonishes you to *"[build] up yourselves on your most holy faith, praying in the Holy Ghost"* (Jude 1:20). Prayer based on God's Word is the key to overcoming the onslaught of the enemy. With the Word, you can bombard the hosts of darkness that contend with you with the aim of shipwrecking your faith and aborting God's purpose for your life. In every contention of your faith, you are to pray (see Luke 18:1).

Through the Blood of Jesus Christ

Apostle John in the Apocalypse declares:

> *"And I heard a loud voice saying in heaven, 'Now is come salvation, and strength, and the kingdom of our God, and the power of his Christ: for the accuser of our brethren is cast down, which accused them before our God day and night. And they overcame him by the blood of the Lamb, and by the word of their testimony; and they loved not their lives unto the death"* (Revelation 12:10-11).

There is inexhaustible and unassailable power in the blood of Jesus Christ. The devil is called the accuser of the brethren and seeks to control and manipulate through guilt and accusations as he aims to blackmail the believer before the Holy God. However, the blood of the Lamb that has been slain speaks on your behalf and causes you to triumph as He responds to Satan's accusations and the onslaught of the enemy.

The blood of Jesus speaks better things than that of Abel. Hebrews 12:24 declares, *"And to Jesus the mediator of the new covenant, and to the blood of sprinkling, that speaketh better things than that of Abel."* Jesus' blood cries out for the forgiveness of your sins, healing of your body, and peace and soundness of your mind. The blood of Jesus is speaking blood, and it is powerful and working on your behalf.

On the contrary, in Genesis 4:8-11, Cain murdered his brother because his offering was unacceptable to the Lord. When the Lord asked him the whereabouts of his brother, he retorted back to the Lord, "Am I my brother's keeper?" The Lord then replied to him saying, "The voice of your brother's blood is crying unto me from the ground." Abel's blood cried out for retribution and vengeance. Understand the power of the voice of Jesus's blood that speaks better things from the mercy seat while that of Abel cries from the ground for the Lord to avenge his death.

When you learn to appropriate the power in the blood of Jesus Christ in faith, you will see the hosts of darkness dismantled and their strategies rendered ineffective against your loved ones and yourself. Do not take for granted the awesome power of the blood of Jesus; use it to your advantage.

Through the Name of Jesus Christ

The scripture declares:

> *"Wherefore God also hath highly exalted him, and given him a name which is above every name: That at the name of Jesus every knee should bow, of things in heaven, and things in earth, and things under the earth; And that every tongue should confess that Jesus Christ is Lord, to the glory of God the Father"* (Philippians 2:9-11).

The above Scriptural text sums it all up. There is power in the name of Jesus Christ. As believers, you have been empowered to use the name of Jesus Christ to contend and engage with the forces that oppose your faith and overthrow it. This is evident in Luke 10:17 as you see the early disciples testify to the power and authority of the name of Jesus. It is an unquestionable fact that you have been given the legal and spiritual right to the use of the name of Jesus, the Christ (see Matthew 28:18-20). Therefore, when you make use of the name of Jesus to contend for your faith, you will begin to experience victory on every side.

Through the Word of our Testimony

"And they overcame him by the blood of the Lamb, and by the word of their testimony; and they loved not their lives unto the death" (Revelation 12:11).

We can contend for the faith when we line up with God's Word and testify to what has been declared about us, rather than agreeing with and attesting to the circumstances and situations in our lives. Every time there are situations in our lives, the enemy wants to hear our testimonies, and if our testimonies do not line up with God's word, he is empowered, given access, and he then gets a foothold into our lives to cause havoc. However, when they line up with the word of God, he is frustrated as you move on to total victory.

EXPLOITS OF FAITH

. . . .

"And what shall I more say? for the time would fail me to tell of Gedeon, and of Barak, and of Samson, and of Jephthae; of David also, and Samuel, and of the prophets: Who through faith subdued kingdoms, wrought righteousness, obtained promises, stopped the mouths of lions, Quenched the violence of fire, escaped the edge of the sword, out of weakness were made strong, waxed valiant in fight, turned to flight the armies of the aliens" (Hebrews 11:32-34).

Our walk of faith can and will produce extraordinary exploits as the above Scriptures make clear. When your faith in God and His Word is adequately appropriated, you will experience tremendous results because the law of faith is universal and timeless. Great exploits such as mentioned in Hebrews 11:32-34 are associated with the patriarchs of old primarily because of their faith in God and obedience to His commands. If you desire to have and experience extraordinary results as the patriarchs of past, it is imperative that you walk the walk of faith just as they did.

Matthew 17:20 further elaborates on the subject of faith, as Jesus reprimands His disciples saying: "Because of your unbelief: for verily I say unto you, If ye have faith as a grain of mustard seed, ye shall say unto this mountain, 'Remove hence to yonder place'; and it shall remove, and nothing shall be impossible unto you." This text indicates that unbelief can rob you of the miracles, blessings, and the great things that God has in store for His children. Consequently, faith, on the other hand, enables you to walk in victory any day, anytime, anywhere. It gives color to your life and empowers you to stand in the midst of oppositions or challenging circumstances and yet be in command, knowing that what He has promised never fails.

The entire eleventh chapter of Hebrews is filled with men and women who through faith did outstanding exploits that glorified God. The verses above state in vivid terms that these men subdued kingdoms, obtained promises, stopped the mouth of lions, quenched the violence of fire, escaped the edge of the sword and so forth through their faith in God and His Word. God is not a respecter of persons, and He is the same yesterday, today, and forever (see Hebrews 13:8). Consequently, if you exercise the same kind of biblical faith and hold onto God's Word as your ultimate guarantee, He will do great and mighty exploits in and through your life in ways that you least expect.

CHARACTERISTICS OF FAITH

What you have often called faith has been a misrepresentation and misconception of the kind of mountain-removing faith portrayed in the Bible. This occurs primarily as a result of lack of knowledge as it relates to the characteristics of faith. Let us examine some of them:

Now: *"Now faith is the substance of things hoped for, the evidence of things not seen"* (Hebrews 11:1).

The verse states, *"Now* faith is." The God-kind of faith is supernatural. It is *now* faith, not yesterday faith. It is the *now* faith that gets things done. For our faith to be operative, it must be the God-kind of faith, supernatural faith, and *now* faith, not yesterday or tomorrow faith. It is faith that is not in any way influenced by things heard, seen, or felt, but it is faith that, on the contrary, influences those ideas and brings them into conformity with its irresistible commands. It operates in the present; it is not something in the distant future, but here and now. The now faith gets answers to prayers - the same faith that brought a dead damsel back to life and handed her back to her mother (see Mark 5:39-42).

Perseverance: *"For a certain woman, whose young daughter had an unclean spirit, heard of him, and came and fell at his feet: The woman was a Greek, a Syrophenician by nation; and she besought him that he would cast forth the devil out of her daughter. But Jesus said unto her, 'Let the children first be filled: for it is not meet to take the children's bread, and to cast it unto the dogs.' And she answered and said unto him, 'Yes, Lord: yet the dogs under the table eat of the children's crumbs.' And he said unto her, 'For this saying go thy way; the devil is gone out of thy daughter'"* (Mark 7:25-29).

These verses of Scripture show us the delicate position of this woman. With Jesus' response to her, one would have expected her to be offended, but she did not let it bother her. She was consistent and determined not to take "NO" for an answer in her quest for a miracle. She knew what she wanted, and there was no doubt in her mind that she would get what she had made up her mind to obtain from Jesus regardless of the challenges that she faced.

Humility: *"The centurion answered and said, 'Lord, I am not worthy that thou shouldest come under my roof: but speak the word only, and my servant shall be healed. For I am a man under authority, having soldiers under me: and I say to this man, "Go," and he goeth; and to another, "Come," and he cometh; and to my servant, "Do this," and he doeth it.' When Jesus heard it, he marvelled, and said to them that followed, 'Verily I say unto you, I have not found so great faith, no, not in Israel'"* (Matthew 8:8-10).

The centurion was a man with military, political, and economic power, yet in spite of his status, he told Jesus that he was not worthy to have Him come under his roof. He had a firm conviction that at the spoken word, his servant would be healed. You see, child of God, humility is not just a faith character, but it is also a virtue. As we submit and humble ourselves under the irrefutable Word of God, we will begin to experience and unleash its power in our lives.

Earnestness: Hebrews 11:6 (NIV) reads: *"And without faith it is impossible to please God, because anyone who comes to him must believe that he exists and that he rewards those who earnestly seek him."*

Earnestness is a function of faith, an attitude characterized by seriousness and commitment, to be intensely, or even excessively earnest and sincere in manner or attitude, ardent in the pursuit of an object, eager to obtain, having a longing desire, warmly engaged or incited. *"And Jesus answered and said unto him, 'What wilt thou that I should do unto thee?' The blind man said unto him, 'Lord, that I might receive my sight'"* (Mark 10:51). This blind man was not uncertain of his needs, but he was earnest and sincere about the request for the restoration of his sight. Most believers engage God and His Word with an attitude that does not characterize earnestness but one that reveals a lack of absolute faith in God and His word as the final arbiter. Faith, therefore, is earnest and has a genuine and severe character as you see in the story of the blind man.

Daringness: *"Now when Daniel knew that the writing was signed, he went into his house; and with his windows being open* *in his chamber toward Jerusalem, he kneeled upon his knees three times a day, and prayed, and gave thanks before his God, as he did aforetime"* (Daniel 6:10).

The story of Daniel in the lions' den shows the daringness of faith. Daniel is raised to a prominent office in the kingdom of Medes and was preferred above his fellows because in him was an excellent spirit. For this reason, jealous rivals sought ways to destroy him, but when they could not find anything against Daniel, the enemies devised a plan that deceived King Darius into issuing and signing into effect the decree that ultimately condemned Daniel to Death.

Daniel knew very well that transgressing the king's decree would attract serious consequences, which would ultimately endanger his life. This development did not deter him from his usual practice of spending time with God. Fear was not his preoccupation because he had a daring faith in God and was prepared to take the risk, trusting the Lord all the way through for a miracle. If you desire to see the hand of the Lord work mightily in and through you, your faith must exhibit this daring character.

FAITH MUST BE TESTED

. . . .

"Wherein ye greatly rejoice, though now for a season, if need be, ye are in heaviness through manifold temptations: That the trial of your faith, being much more precious than of gold that perisheth, though it be tried with fire, might be found unto praise and honour and glory at the appearing of Jesus Christ:" (1 Peter 1:6-7).

The testing of faith is the means through which the genuineness of faith is proven, and your motivations revealed. The trial of faith also helps the Christian character to develop, as clearly elucidated in James 1:2-4, which states, *"My brethren, count it all joy when ye fall into divers temptations; Knowing this, that the trying of your faith worketh patience. But let patience have her perfect work, that ye may be perfect and entire, wanting nothing."* God's Word is filled with examples of men and women whose faith was tested.

One of many such examples was Abraham whom God asked to sacrifice his son, Isaac, his only son whom he had waited for a long time into his old age when it was seemingly physically impossible to have a child (see Genesis 22:1-2 & Hebrews 11:17-19 respectively). This suffices to say that it is your tested faith that positions you to receive the promises of God's Word and enables you to experience and to unleash the power of God in your life. When you go through challenges, consider them as refining and testing your faith. As your faith goes through the test, you will undoubtedly experience God's Word as your guarantee that He will perfect all that concerns you.

FAITH VERSUS FEAR

. . . .

Faith will activate the power of God in and through your life to overcome your circumstances and live a triumphant life in God. Faith in God's Word is the victory that enables you to overcome the world (see 1 John 5:4). It is what brings about the manifestations of God's provisions from the spiritual realm into the physical realm (see Ephesians 1:3). Everything God did for you is by grace through Christ Jesus and must be accessed through faith in Him and His Word. In Hebrews 11:6, the Scriptures say,

> *"But without faith it is impossible to please Him: for he that cometh to God must believe that he is, and that he is a rewarder of them that diligently seek him"* (Hebrews 11:6).

Understanding the sequence in the Scriptural text above will enable you to accurately appropriate God's Word that guarantees victories over the forces of sickness, disease, poverty, and wickedness of any kind. As you receive and appropriate God's Word in your life, you will begin to possess your God-given inheritance, maximizing your potential and fulfilling destiny.

The sequence is as follows

1. You must come to God.
2. You must believe that He is; that He is the "I am that I am" [the self-existent God].
3. Know that God is a rewarder.
4. You must be a diligent seeker.

This implies that faith activates God's favor upon your life and as you are favored of the Lord; impossibilities become possibilities. Fear, on the other hand, will enable the power of the devil in your life and disconnect you from the life of God. The devil's trick is *fear*, which is to make *false evidence appear real* to you, which will, of course, paralyze and disorient you, putting you in what I call spiritual incarceration. If fear goes undetected and disarmed, it will bring about severe consequences in your life. Therefore, let me submit to you that faith is based on God's Word, while fear is based on your circumstances and insecurities.

Fear: "The Devil's Tool"

. . . .

"Why is light given to a man whose way is hid, and whom God hath hedged in? For my sighing cometh before I eat, and my roarings are poured out like the waters. For the thing which I greatly feared is come upon me, and that which I was afraid of is come unto me" (Job 3:23-25).

When you examine the above passage, you will discover that Brother Job appears to have been entertaining fear in his heart before the devil's assault on his life and his entire household.

Understand this one thing: that the devil knew he would not have been able to besiege Job and his whole family, as long as the hedge of protection was in place and undamaged. Fear, therefore, is one of the primary weapons of the devil in assaulting the believer in Christ, and he knows very well that fear exposes you and makes you vulnerable to his attacks. In the devil's discussion with God, he said,

> *"Hast not thou made an hedge about him, and about his house, and about all that he hath on every side? thou hast blessed the work of his hands, and his substance is increased in the land"* (Job 1:10).

This suggestively postulates that the devil had tried in so many ways and supposedly at different times to destroy Job's life only to discover that there was a hedge roundabout him.

The Scripture lets us understand that

> *"As the mountains are round about Jerusalem, so the LORD is round about his people from henceforth even for ever"* (Psalms 125:2).

Job was ignorant of this timeless truth as many believers are today. As long as the hedge of protection is a roundabout you and you are walking by faith and in obedience to God's Word, know that the devil understands that he cannot touch you or anything that concerns you.

What Is a Hedge?

Let us start by finding out what the word "hedge" means. According to the Merriam-Webster Collegiate Dictionary, hedge means "a means of protection or defense." It also implies "to enclose or protect with." The Hebrew word for "hedge" is *Gadar* (Strong's H1443), which means "to surround with a fence or wall, to wall in or around an enclosure with the purpose of protection or to keep out intruders or enemies."

The devil knew very well that the Lord built a hedge of protection about Job and his entire household and there was nothing he could do to break that hedge. For God specifically said the devil could not touch or harm Job because he was the most righteous man in the land (see Job 1:6-12), so the devil introduced Job to fear. And Job yielding to fear caused the hedge to be broken, giving access to that old serpent, the devil, who immediately took advantage and struck. God's word declares, *"He that diggeth a pit shall fall into it; and whoso breaketh a hedge, a serpent shall bite him"* (Ecclesiastes 10:8). The hedge of protection around Job and his entire family was broken through fear, and as a result, the devil had access to their lives.

This is still the scheme the devil uses against the children of God today, trying to get believers to curse God and doubt His Word. If only you keep on living by faith, that hedge that God has over you will remain intact, making it impossible for any onslaught of the devil to prosper. Please, do not be ignorant of this simple truth for the devil knows this, so he makes false evidence appear real to crack that hedge. Beloved, keep that hedge secure, walking and living daily by faith in God's Word.

From the examples, you see of the children of Israel, as they succumbed to fear, doubt, and unbelief, their actions based on fear unquestionably resulted in the hedge of protection being broken or the presence of the Lord lifting. Inevitably, this led to the following consequences:

- Continual satanic harassment
- Invasion by demonic powers
- The ruin of fruit, labor, and sacrifices
- The enemy being able to establish strongholds
- Opportunities for deception

Your responsibility is to keep that hedge over your life and your household by walking in harmony with the Word of God, and you will be sure that God's Word will be your ultimate guarantee.

CHAPTER 6

ON WHAT FOUNDATION ARE YOU BUILT?

"If the foundations be destroyed, what can the righteous do?" (Psalms 11:3).

"Therefore thus saith the Lord GOD, 'Behold, I lay in Zion for a foundation a stone, a tried stone, a precious corner stone, a sure foundation: he that believeth shall not make haste'"(Isaiah 28:16)

WHAT IS A FOUNDATION?

. . . .

Webster's Revised Unabridged Dictionary 1913 defines foundation as "That, upon which anything is founded; that on which anything stands, and by which it is supported; the lowest and supporting layer of a superstructure; groundwork; basis."

A foundation, therefore, is a bedrock, a structure, a strong, stable base on which a building is erected. Foundations are the essential part of any building, no matter how magnificent or splendid the edifice may be. When we talk about a foundation, church builders, civil engineers, architects and other professionals in the construction industry are well acquainted with this word because of its importance and inevitability. The foundation on which a building is constructed will determine the size, the strength, and the weight that the structure can support and its durability under pressure. It is imperative to understand that one can never build more significantly than the foundation can handle, so proper attention must be given and quality time spent laying a solid foundation.

Apostle Paul elaborated the critical nature of a foundation when he said:

> *"Now if any man build upon this foundation gold, silver, precious stones, wood, hay, stubble; Every man's work shall be made manifest: for the day shall declare it, because it shall be revealed by fire; and the fire shall try every man's work of what sort it is. If any man's work abides which he hath built thereupon, he shall receive a reward. If any man's work shall be burned, he shall suffer loss: but he himself shall be saved; yet so as by fire"* (1 Corinthians 3:12-15).

The text above makes the importance of laying the right foundation explicitly and entirely clear. We must, therefore, take into consideration what kind of foundation we are laying and on what foundation we are building. For as the Scriptures state, every man's work shall be tested.

TWO KINDS OF FOUNDATIONS
· ·

"Whosoever cometh to me, and heareth my sayings, and doeth them, I will shew you to whom he is like: He is like a man which built a house, and dug deep, and laid the foundation on a rock: and when the flood

arose, the stream beat vehemently upon that house, and could not shake it: for it was founded upon a rock. But he that heareth, and doeth not, is like a man that without a foundation built an house upon the earth; against which the stream did beat vehemently, and immediately it fell; and the ruin of that house was great" (Luke 6:47-49).

The Greek word for "*foundation*" is *Themélios* (Strong's G2310,) meaning a "substruction (of a building)." Jesus here speaks of two kinds of foundations: the foundation laid on *the rock (The Word)* and the foundation laid on *earth (sand, natural reasoning, and emotions)*. The same structure can be laid on each of these foundations, but which of the foundations it is built on will determine the strength and durability of the structure.

The foundation laid on the rock is one that results from hearing and doing God's Word, while the foundation laid on the earth occurs from hearing without acting on the Word of God. In James 1:22, the Apostle James admonishes us to be "*doers of the word, and not hearers only.*" It is crucial for us to understand if we are to build on the rock that cannot fail; we must "do" the Word and not just hear it.

The above story is also recorded in Matthew 7:24-27 where Jesus Christ calls the man that builds his foundation upon the rock a *wise* man while the man that builds upon the earth He calls a *foolish* man. What brings about the difference between the wise and the foolish? To be wise here is not about your age or the countless number of grey hairs on your head. To be wise is becoming a hearer *and* a doer of the Word of God while to be foolish is to be a hearer and *not* a doer of God's Word.

The church today is full of both the wise and the foolish. The wise are not necessarily the ones with beautiful edifices, but those who, after the storms of life have come and gone, have their structures still standing strong directly because their foundation is laid on the rock. When the storms of life beat upon a man whose foundation is built upon the rock, his edifice remains standing and strong. It may be startling to know that most believers do not fall into the category of the wise who have experienced and are still experiencing the prevailing power of God's Word in their lives. However, most believers are not experiencing the power of God not because God doesn't want to show them this power but because they lack the faith to trust God enough to experience His power.

FIRM FOUNDATION

As evidenced in the Bible, a foundation upon the rock, the Word, is a firm and an immovable foundation. Christian believers with this kind of foundation are those who have taken their time to hear and put into practice what they have heard. And they do so by digging deep, in reflection, beyond the surface of the Word of God until they hit the depths and riches of the Word. No matter how sophisticated your building is, if the foundation is not laid on the rock (the Word), in moments of trial, the structure and its foundation will be blown away.

As believers, we can build a firm foundation on the rock by taking heed to and doing the Word. What we have today are many hearers and talkers of God's Word, but few hearers and doers. What brings results is not just the hearing and talking, but the hearing and *doing* of the Word. If, as a believer, you have been hearing and speaking without doing, I strongly suggest that you start doing the Word today.

THE ROCK (THE WORD)

When considering laying a foundation, a builder needs to look closely at the kind of structure he wants to build and how strong the foundation needs to be to sustain the structure. A structure or building can look beautiful, but the strength of the foundation is what ultimately determines the strength and durability of the structure. If the foundation on which a structure is laid is superficial, peril and disaster are imminent.

The Word of God makes it clear that the man or woman whose structure does not collapse under adverse conditions has laid his/her foundation upon the rock. It is therefore evident that such a man/woman has taken time to hear and apply that which has been heard, which is laying the foundation on the rock. This implies that an improperly laid foundation endangers the structure that is erected on it, irrespective of how magnificent that structure or edifice may look.

It appears that this situation is so prevalent in Christendom today. We have lovely Christians with magnificent structures, who talk right, comb right, dress right, are tongue talkers, and do all the "rights," but when the onslaught of the enemy causes offense, they break down and are washed away by the floods of life just like that house whose foundation was laid upon the earth. The reason is that many Christians run along hearing God's Word without doing the Word, just as the parable of the sower teaches us: *"he who received the seed on stony places, this is he who hears the word and immediately receives it with joy; yet he has no root in himself, but endures only for a while. For when tribulation or persecution arises because of the word, immediately he stumbles"* (Matthew 13:20-21 NKJV).

These people hear the Word, receive it with gladness and excitement, but it only endures for a season as the enemy attacks the hearer before the Word takes root in the hearer. This causes the hearer to stumble because that foundation was laid on just excitement and feelings. Apostle Paul declares in Colossians 3:16 that we should *"Let the Word of Christ dwell in you richly."*

You see, the Word of God ought to be the foundation on which our lives are built, for God's Word will prevail against any onslaught of the enemy. Thank God for His Word is forever settled in Heaven; Glory to God! Perhaps the reason why you have not been able to overcome that enemy, secret sin, disease, poverty, or lust is that your foundation is not laid on the unchanging, unmovable, and unbreakable Rock - God's Word. Examine and change your foundation accordingly today, and your life will never be the same.

How to Build a Strong Foundation

. . . .

Study God's Word

To build a strong foundation, you must take heed to the admonition of Apostle Paul to Timothy: *"Study to shew thyself approved unto God, a workman that needeth not to be ashamed, rightly dividing the word of truth"* (2 Timothy 2:15).

God's Word is the mind of God and His will for us. As you study the Word of God, you are being acquainted with the mind and will of God for your life, and as you continue in the Word, you build a solid foundation of the Word in your life. God's Word helps renew your mind, which in turn affects your thought-life that will ultimately determine the choices and decisions you make. This will eventually help you build the right foundation.

Meditate on God's Word

Joshua 1:8 reads: *"This book of the law shall not depart out of thy mouth; but thou shalt meditate therein day and night, that thou mayest observe to do according to all that is written therein: for then thou shalt make thy way prosperous, and then thou shalt have good success."*

To meditate means, to care for, to attend to, and to ponder. Meditating God's Word helps us build a solid foundation in various aspects of our lives. Likewise, Apostle Paul says, *"Let the word of Christ dwell in you richly in all wisdom; teaching and admonishing one another in psalms and hymns and spiritual songs, singing with grace in your hearts to the Lord* (Colossians 3:16). Meditation on the Word of God causes God's word to "dwell in you" and become a source of wisdom in your mind, will, and emotions, helping you build a solid foundation in your walk of faith.

Apply God's Word

To build a strong foundation, the practical application of God's Word cannot be overstated. Apostle James declares, *"But be ye doers of the word, and not hearers only, deceiving your own selves"* (James 1:22). Applying God's Word is a critical component of building a strong foundation in your walk with God. The doers of God's Word are those who are governed by it, who essentially conform to its requirements, who not only read, understand, and believe it but also submit to its counsel and authority and live by its instructions. It is the Word of God heard, received, and acted upon that produces lasting results and helps build a strong foundation.

Pray in the Holy Ghost

"But ye, beloved, building up yourselves on your most holy faith, praying in the Holy Ghost" (Jude 1:20). As we pray in the language of the Spirit, this spiritual exercise helps us build a strong foundation. Apostle Paul states that when we do not pray as we ought to pray, the Holy Spirit helps our inability to pray right and this He does through us praying in the Holy Ghost (see Romans 8:26).

Fellowship

The Scripture admonishes that we should not forsake the assembly of the brethren. This is a critical point in building a strong foundation. Solomon lets us understand in Proverbs 27:17 that *"Iron sharpeneth iron; so a man sharpeneth the countenance of his friend."* As we fellowship with one another, we interact with our minds, sharing a different perspective of God's Word, experiences, and testimonies, thus, strengthening one another and gleaning wisdom that will help facilitate building a firm foundation.

Keep Good Company

The company you keep or the people you get along with will go a long way to determining the type of foundation you dig, and how you erect the building. Apostle Paul observes in 1 Corinthians 15:33, *"Be not deceived: evil communications corrupt good manners."* The company that you keep or associate with will cause you either total success or total ruin. Therefore, keeping the right company is imperative to building a strong and lasting foundation.

Seek Godly Counsel

Human advice is desirable, but not always reliable. Only God's counsel is wholly dependable. Hence, in all matters of life, seeking godly counsel is of the utmost importance. The Scriptures say, *"Where no counsel is, the people fall: but in the multitude of counsellors there is safety"* (Proverbs 11:14). The Scriptures explicitly give us the blueprint for making wise decisions—openly seek godly counsel on matters and then apply it. As people, we are bound to fail and fall without appropriate advice or guidance in any aspect of our lives.

In our walk of faith, the answers to all our questions are found in the Scriptures. How often do we consult them? How often do we seek counsel before making significant decisions in our lives? Consequently, in building a solid foundation, godly counsel must be sought after and heeded. I cannot stress this enough (see also Proverbs 15:22). It is sad to note that there are people who never seek or give heed to godly counsel and this has led to avoidable mistakes in their lives. Take heed to what the Word of God declares: *"The way of a fool is right in his own eyes, but a wise man listens to advice"* (Proverbs 12:15 ESV).

CHAPTER 7

HOPE AGAINST HOPE

WHAT IS HOPE?

. . . .

"For I know the thoughts that I think toward you, saith the LORD, thoughts of peace, and not of evil, to give you an expected end" (Jeremiah 29:11)

"Hope" is the Hebrew word *Tiqvah* (Strong's H8615), meaning "expectation; something yearned for and anticipated eagerly; something for which one waits." *Tiqvah* comes from the verb *Qâvâh* (Strong's H6960), meaning "to tarry" or "to wait for" or "to look hopefully" in a particular direction, an expectation, something yearned for with anticipated eagerness. Hope, therefore, is not inferior to faith as we are made to believe most of the time but it is an extension of faith. Without hope, which is the expectation, faith has no basis on which to work.

"Hope deferred maketh the heart sick: but when the desire cometh, it is a tree of life" (Proverbs 13:12).

It is imperative to understand that hope deferred births discouragement and unbelief, but the hope realized becomes a tree of life that produces excellent things such as healing, prosperity, joy and much more in your life. Hope creates unending tenacity to hold on to our God-given purpose in life and the promises of God that are yea and amen. Hope builds constant capacity to trust God and believe He can do the impossible.

Consequently, faith is the present possession of things hoped for, not yet seen, while on the other hand, hope is the confident expectation and accomplishment of things not seen. Therefore, hope is not an optimistic outlook or wishful thinking without any foundation, but it is the confident expectation based on solid certainty. Scriptural hope consequently rests on God's promises as stated in His Word.

HOPE COMES THROUGH GOD'S WORD

. . . .

"Who against hope believed in hope, that he might become the father of many nations, according to that which was spoken..." (Romans 4:18).

The Apostle Paul reveals to us in the above Scriptural text that Abraham "against hope believed in hope." What does this mean? "Against hope" implies against all human expectation, or apparent possibility, and "believed in hope" signifies that Abraham believed that God's promise would undoubtedly take place despite the human improbability. As we study the Scriptures precisely, we discover that there were natural hope and supernatural hope evident in Abraham's situation.

The natural kind of hope is that which comes as a result of facts, all the arguments of logical reasoning and experience that are evident in the natural world. In our discourse, we will refer to this as **negative hope**. The fact was that Abraham and Sarah were unable to have children because they had long passed the age of childbearing, but against all the evidence, he believed in hope: the hope that one day he would become the father of many nations as spoken by God, understanding that his situation was beyond human hopes, but in spite of that he rested it upon hope in God.

The supernatural kind of hope is that which comes as a result of God's Word and His omnipotence. It was this kind of hope that enabled Abraham to see beyond natural inducement based upon conscious perceptions to God's all-sufficiency and the hope of becoming the father of many nations, according to God's Word and by faith, seeing the promise fulfilled in Sarah, his wife; this I will term *positive hope.*

Abraham and Sarah were well advanced in age, and Sarah had passed the age of childbearing (see Genesis 18:11), a hopeless situation with clear evidence to prove it. This situation gave negative hope of the impossibility of ever having a child, as it was excessively late by human standards. God spoke to Abraham promising him a son, and positive hope was born in his heart, which explains why the Scripture uses the words "against hope" (negative hope or natural hope based on the arguments of the senses that saw having a baby as physically impossible).

Abraham believed in hope (positive hope), that which sees what God says as possible, knowing that it would surely happen, irrespective of the present circumstances (the deadness of Sarah's womb). The Scripture attests to this when it declares "Through faith also Sara herself received strength to conceive seed, and was delivered of a child when she was past age because she judged him faithful who had promised" (Hebrews 11:11).

You may have lost hope in your situation, but you have to understand that one word from God can change the situation for your good (see Romans 8:28). Where everything else fails, God's Word cannot fail, for God watches over His word to perform it, and His Word is forever settled in Heaven. Consider this, Child of God: the Scripture declares in Romans 4:19-22, *"And being not weak in faith, he considered not his own body now dead, when he was about an hundred years old, neither yet the deadness of Sarah's womb: He staggered not at the promise of God through unbelief; but was strong in faith, giving glory to God; And being fully persuaded that, what he had promised, he was able also to perform. And therefore it was imputed to him for righteousness."*

Weak faith results from giving consideration or meditation to the circumstances with which we are faced. To have strong faith, we must stay focused on God's Word as the final arbiter of all life situations. Unbelief is at the root of our staggering at the promises of God, and it leads to double-mindedness (see James 8) and instability in our hearts. Strong faith is born as we stay focused on God's promises without wavering and with the ardent persuasion that God can do exceedingly, abundantly, above all that we may ask or think according to the power that works in us. God's Word brings hope to the hopeless as the Word is received and acted upon in spite of circumstances.

When hope is lost, it means that the confident expectation and accomplishment of things not seen have been exchanged with impossibility, which is now based on the experiences of the natural senses. Be it sickness, poverty or an impossible situation in which you have lost hope, the first thing to do is to submit to God's Word and discover for yourself what He has said. This will restore hope to you irrespective of the situation. You may have a situation that seems hopeless, but I want you to rest assured that one Word from God can make a great difference in your life.

The dilemma of most Christians is that often they confess faith in the absence of hope. It does not work that way; "faith is the substance of the things hoped for, the evidence of things not seen" (see Hebrews 11:1). Therefore, it's of utmost importance that you have hope for something for faith to act upon and obtain that, which was expected. Like faith, hope must be based on God and His Word to achieve results, for when your hope is anchored on God's Word, there will be a performance, and a physical manifestation of the things hoped for. Understand that something seen is not hope, which is a firm assurance and expectation of things not seen. When something manifests, it is no longer hope.

THE HOPE OF FULFILMENT
VERSUS GOD'S DEMAND

·······················

"And it came to pass after these things, that God did tempt Abraham, and said unto him, 'Abraham': and he said, 'Behold, here I am.' And he said, 'Take now thy son, thine only son Isaac, whom thou lovest, and get thee into the land of Moriah; and offer him there for a burnt offering upon one of the mountains which I will tell thee of.' And Abraham rose up early in the morning, and saddled his ass, and took two of his young men with him, and Isaac his son, and clave the wood for the burnt offering, and rose up, and went unto the place of which God had told him" (Genesis 22:1-3).

The hope of fulfillment cannot be circumvented by God's demands, but instead, it consolidates and strengthens the accomplishment of that which He says. After Isaac, the son of promise, was born, God asked Abraham to sacrifice him. This was an incredible and strange request for a man who had waited so long to have a child. Knowing that it was through this child that the promise of becoming the father of many nations was to be accomplished would have made God's demands to sacrifice the child of promise seem utterly ridiculous.

However, Abraham's hope was not built on illusions but the integrity of God's Word, knowing that God cannot back down on His Word. The covenant bond between them was so strong that he obeyed God's request. As it were, it would have run through Abraham's mind that sacrificing his son could retard or destroy the hope of the fulfillment of God's promise upon his life and his entire generation. In addition, having waited for such an extended period before Isaac was born, Abraham would have been skeptical about God's request.

However, the Scriptures declare in Hebrews 11:19, "[Abraham] *accounting that God was able to raise him, even from the dead; from whence also he received him in a figure."* This text tells us that Abraham was fully persuaded that God was able to raise his son, Isaac, from the dead if it got to the point of offering his only son as a sacrifice as demanded by God.

Therefore, the subject of non-fulfillment of the promise of God to him was beside the point. When your hope is genuinely predicated on God's word, you will be willing to sacrifice all your Isaacs (precious things) to God to please Him without considering whether His promises will be accomplished in your life. When God asks us to put our Isaacs on the altar, He gives us the privilege to experience Him as our sole provider (Jehovah Jireh).

CHAPTER 8

LIVING IN THE AUTHORITY OF GOD'S WORD

"Forever, O Lord, thy word is settled in heaven" (Psalms 119:89).

"For as the rain cometh down, and the snow from heaven, and returneth not thither, but watereth the earth, and maketh it bring forth and bud, that it may give seed to the sower, and bread to the eater: So shall my word be that goeth forth out of my mouth: it shall not return unto me void, but it shall accomplish that which I please, and it shall prosper in the thing whereto I sent it" (Isaiah 55:10-11).

In the verses above, David bears witness to the truth that the word of God is forever settled in Heaven. This is good news irrespective of what we go through here on earth. Our circumstances can neither change nor alter the counsel of God's Word concerning you and me, for His Word is forever settled. The prophet Isaiah further stresses the authority of God's Word and reveals to us that God's Word cannot return to Him void until it accomplishes that which the Lord pleases and prospers in its purposes. Living in the authority of God's Word is the sure way to experiencing the God-kind of life we were created to live.

Nevertheless, most believers are not living and experiencing the authority of God's Word, and this is a sad situation because the enemy wages war against us daily, on every side. The need for the church to live and experience the authority of God's Word in every area of life more than ever before cannot be overemphasized. It is imperative for us as children of God to recognize that it is God's will for us to live in harmony and in the authority of His Word. Living in the authority of God's Word is a matter of appropriating kingdom principles. It will not just happen because we name the name of Jesus Christ, or because we are members of a particular local assembly. The Word of God works when we work God's Word. There are specific dynamics that must be built into our lives to activate the authority of God's Word in our everyday lives.

How to Activate the Authority of God's Word

. . . .

By Faith

"When Jesus heard it, he marvelled, and said to them that followed, 'Verily I say unto you, I have not found so great faith, no, not in Israel'" (Matthew 8:10).

The question is not whether God's Word possesses authority but rather how can you have access to that authority? It is by faith that you can appropriate the authority of God's Word. Exercising faith in God's Word authorizes us to draw strength and power from God. Apostle Paul states, *"But without faith it is impossible to please him: for he that cometh to God must believe that he is, and that he is a rewarder of them that diligently seek him"* (Hebrews 11: 6). Here, the Scripture makes it clear that without faith it is impossible to please God.

The Gospel of Matthew further elucidates, *"And Jesus said unto the centurion, 'Go thy way; and as thou hast believed, so be it done unto thee.' And his servant was healed in the selfsame hour"* (Matthew 8:13). Child of God, your ability to live and experience the authority of God's Word is predicated on this simple but yet profound statement: *"as thou hast believed, so be it done unto thee."* This is good news. You may have conditions or situations that have defied all human solutions, but no matter what your condition is in life, you can live in the authority of God's Word by believing what God's Word says concerning your situation.

Remember the story of the two blind men. Jesus said, *"According to your faith be it unto you"* (Matthew 9:29). These blind men were living and experiencing the authority of God's Word to the degree of their faith. You too will live and experience the authority of God's Word to the degree of your faith. It is by faith in the Word of God that we experience the authority of God's Word. Apostle Paul remarks in Romans 10:17, *"So then faith cometh by hearing, and hearing by the word of God."* Simply articulated, faith is produced by hearing and hearing by the Word of God, and we must walk by faith and not by what we see. Fear, as opposed to faith, will cause you not to live and experience the authority of God's Word (Matthew 14:22-31).

Through Confession

"For with the heart man believeth unto righteousness; and with the mouth confession is made unto salvation" (Romans 10:10).

Most believers who are defeated in life are defeated because they believe and confess the wrong things. Proverbs 6:2 says, *"Thou art snared with the words of thy mouth..."* The Greek word for *"confess"* is *Homologeo* (Strong's G3670), and it is a compound word comprising *Homoû* (Strong's G3674), meaning "same, together with," and *Lego* (Strong's G3004), meaning, "to speak, to say, to assent, to consent." *Homologeo*, therefore, means, "to speak the same thing as another, to agree with or to acknowledge, to adopt the same style of speech, to speak alike, to agree with or consent to the desire of another." Concerning the believers' confession, "homologeo" means, "saying the same thing God says, speaking according to His Word." Unfortunately, most believers have only been taught the confession of their wrongdoings before God, which is a good practice for every child of God. However, we must go beyond confession as solely a tool for confessing our sins but also for declaring consistently what the Word of God says about us.

Irrespective of your situation, you must learn to speak in accordance to what God's Word has declared concerning you and when you do this, you are setting in motion the authority of God's Word in your life. Acting contrary to His Word will be counterproductive now and hereafter. There is a dimension to confessing God's Word; it is not just about verbalizing the words but also believing in your heart that what God said is so and it shall be so.

> *"Let us hold fast the profession of our faith without wavering; (for he is faithful that promised;)" (Hebrews 10:23).*

By the Spoken Word of God

> *"The centurion answered and said, 'Lord, I am not worthy that thou shouldest come under my roof: but speak the word only, and my servant shall be healed.'"*
> *"When the even was come, they brought unto him many that were possessed with devils: and he cast out the spirits with his word, and healed all that were sick:" (Matthew 8:8, 16).*

Here we see the power of the spoken word in action. The centurion sought help from Jesus for his servant that was paralyzed and dreadfully tormented. Jesus responded saying, "I will come and heal him" (see Matthew 8:16). The Centurion understood what it meant to live in the authority of the spoken word. The Centurion's response in the above-mentioned Scriptural text infers that Jesus did not need to come to his house for his servant's need to be met because he had experienced the authority of the spoken word personally as a man under authority. He said when I say to one go, he goes, and when I say to one come, he comes." He said to Jesus, "*...but speak the word only, and my servant shall be healed.*"

You can only see the manifestation of the authority of God's Word when spoken and declared in faith. The centurion believed in the authority of God's Word and experienced its manifestation. In like manner, you and I can experience and live in the authority of God's Word when spoken in faith. The story recounted in Luke 5:5, shows that Peter also understood the authority of the spoken Word of God. He says to Jesus, "*Master, we have toiled all the night, and have taken nothing: nevertheless at thy word I will let down the net.*" Though it seemed improbable that they would take anything after having toiled all night in vain, yet Peter was willing to trust the *Word* of Jesus, and on that day, he experienced a great catch.

> "*And Jesus answering saith unto them, 'Have faith in God.' For verily I say unto you, 'That whosoever shall say unto this mountain, "Be thou removed, and be thou cast into the sea"; and shall not doubt in his heart, but shall believe that those things which he saith shall come to pass; he shall have whatsoever he saith*" (Mark 11:22-23).

Here, we see Jesus explaining a divine truth to His disciples. In the text above, our Lord Jesus teaches His disciples to have the God-kind of faith and this faith is manifested in the spoken word. When we say to this mountain be moved and cast into the sea without a doubt in our hearts, it shall be so. What mountain are you confronted with today? You do not have to whine and complain but speak the Word of God in faith, and that mountain shall dissipate.

By Walking in the Spirit

In his letter to the Galatian Church, Apostle Paul states: *"This I say then, 'Walk in the Spirit, and ye shall not fulfill the lust of the flesh'"* (Galatians 5:16). To walk in the Spirit infers yielding to the influence, direction, and guidance of the Spirit of God. As we submit to the Holy Spirit's power in our lives, we are empowered to overcome the evil propensities of the flesh. We can experience and live in the authority of God's Word by walking in the Spirit.

Now, walking in the Spirit at seldom times does not indicate some of the ridiculous formalities and worldliness that prevail in Christendom. It merely means walking by God's Word, taking heed to the unadulterated Word of God, for God's Word is spirit and life; therefore, walking in the Word is walking in the Spirit. The Scripture declares that the "letter killeth but the Spirit giveth life" (see 2 Corinthians 3:6). It is imperative to walk in the Spirit in order to live in the authority of God's Word. That is, every circumstance of life must be viewed in the light of Scriptures as the final authority even if it is not convenient for the flesh.

By Prayer

"And he spake a parable unto them to this end, that men ought always to pray, and not to faint;" (Luke 18:1).

"Pray without ceasing" (1 Thessalonians 5:17).

The Scripture admonishes us to pray and not faint. Hence, to live in the authority of God's Word, prayer is an unmatched prerequisite and must become part of our daily lifestyles. Oswald Chambers observes, "We have to pray with our eyes on God, not on the difficulties." Unlike the popular opinion that prayer is cumbersome, it can be an enjoyable process that yields outstanding results that can affect you personally, bringing lasting changes to your circumstances. Prayer creates a hunger for God's Word and sensitivity to its instructions.

By Taking Action

The Scriptures teach us in James 1:22 and 2:26 respectively, *"But be ye doers of the word, and not hearers only, deceiving your own selves,"* and *"For as the body without the spirit is dead, so faith without works is dead also."* You must be *doers* of the Word of God to experience its authority. Living in the authority of God's Word demands that you take consistent action: action predicated on the knowledge of His Word.

Please, understand, child of God, that knowledge does not become fruitful until you *act* upon what you know. Your actions must be congruent with your confession and what you believe in your heart. It will prove unfruitful if your actions are not in harmony with what you say with your mouth and what your heart believes. This is one of the reasons why many people are not living and experiencing the authority of God's Word today.

The Word works if you will work the Word and one Word from God can turn your life around immeasurably. When you understand biblical principles and apply them accurately, there will be no doubt that you will live and experience the authority of the Word of God in every aspect of your life. Do not allow ignorance of the Word of God rob you of your access to the authority of God's Word.

CHAPTER 9

KEEPING YOUR THOUGHTS ALIGNED WITH GOD'S WORD

"For though we walk in the flesh, we do not war after the flesh: (For the weapons of our warfare are not carnal, but mighty through God to the pulling down of strong holds;) Casting down imaginations, and every high thing that exalteth itself against the knowledge of God, and bringing into captivity every thought to the obedience of Christ;" (2 Corinthians 10:3-5).

"Finally, brethren, whatsoever things are true, whatsoever things are honest, whatsoever things are just, whatsoever things are pure, whatsoever things are lovely, whatsoever things are of good report; if there be any virtue, and if there be any praise, think on these things" (Philippians 4:8).

The word *"thought"* is the Greek word *Nóēma* (Strong's G3540), which means "a perception, the intellect, disposition, mind, or thought." It also implies "evil thinking/purpose; the act of thinking; the exercise of the mind in any of its higher forms; reflection." We are continually subjected to things that probably like to control, sabotage, and abort our pursuit of God and our God-given destinies. The systems of this world bombard us from every side with negativity and mind-numbing events all day long, which challenge us on every side. This has adverse effects on our thought processes. If we wish to stay afloat through all these things without losing our minds and maintain our sanity and faith in God's Word, we must learn to keep our thoughts synchronized with God's Word daily.

In the book of Psalms 94:11, David declares: *"The LORD knoweth the thoughts of man, that they are vanity."* It is imperative to understand that the inherent thoughts of man are vain and vile without God. These are thoughts that seek nothing but to satisfy the flesh and its desires. Consequently, it is essential to align your thoughts with God's Word daily so that you can ascertain the thoughts of God in whatever situation you find yourself.

The Apostle Paul indicates, *"for though we walk in the flesh, we do not wage war after the flesh:"* (2 Corinthians 10:3). It is important to understand this because most of the battles that the enemy will wage against you will be waged in the realm of your mind, which is the seat of your thoughts, will, and emotions. Your mind is a critical aspect of your life if you want to experience God's Word as your ultimate guarantee.

"The thoughts of the diligent tend only to plenteousness; but of every one that is hasty only to want" (Proverb 21:5). The enemy is well prepared to cause you to be hasty, cast doubt in your mind, and make you believe a lie as the truth. Once he has achieved, gained control of, and distorted your thought life, he will launch the most vicious attack on you and everything that concerns you. You must not allow this to happen by protecting your mind.

The importance of keeping your thoughts aligned with God's Word is one of the critical elements to you walking in total victory.

Solomon declares in Proverbs 23:7, *"For as he thinketh in his heart, so is he: 'Eat and drink,' saith he to thee; but his heart is not with thee."* You are a summation of your thoughts. In other words, you are what you think; your thoughts determine your actions, and your thoughts can bring great success or complete failure. If your thoughts are so important in who you ultimately become, why then is it that most people do not give attention to them? Here is what David has to say in Psalms 139:23: *"Search me, O God, and know my heart: try me, and know my thoughts:"* This should be our everyday prayer that God may reveal the intents of our thoughts so that we can align those thoughts with God's Word daily.

WHAT IS A THOUGHT?

In its simplest form a thought is:

- A mental conception
- The attention of the mind
- An association of ideas
- Silent contemplation
- Inward reasoning

Thoughts are like Seeds: Seeds have the potential to reproduce after their kind. In other words, your thoughts will reproduce after their kind. The question is, what kind of thoughts do you have every day? Are they thoughts of defeat, failure, poverty, and victory or are they more than enough? To think the type of thoughts that will produce the God-kind of life you desire, you have to align your thoughts with God's Word in spite of your circumstances and situation. Changing your thoughts change your perspective which changes how you act in the world.

Suggestions: Thoughts are like suggestions that affect your actions. They flood and inundate your mind so much so that your actions interpret these thoughts. These suggestions can be positive or negative, and the ones we allow to dominate are the ones that control what we do and don't do. Therefore, living out the will of God necessitates you scrutinizing, submitting to, and bringing into alignment these suggestions so that they conform to the will of God for your life.

Images: Sometimes thoughts also come in the form of pictures in your mind. These mental images are the way you see and think about yourself in any given situation. However, when formed, these images are often translated into thoughts and then into actions. It is vital that the image you have of yourself or your circumstances originate from God's Word and not what you perceive of your outer world.

THE SIGNIFICANCE OF ALIGNING YOUR THOUGHTS WITH GOD'S WORD

· ·

"Commit thy works unto the LORD, and thy thoughts shall be established" (Proverbs 16:3)

Everything we do, everything we say starts with a thought. Our emotions and feelings are generated from an initial thought in our minds. Aligning your thoughts with God's Word implies subjecting your thoughts to God's Word and bringing into captivity every thought that wants to exalt itself above the knowledge of God's Word in your life and turning it in obedience to Christ (see 2 Corinthians 10:5). Therefore, the issue of aligning your thoughts with God's Word becomes a subject matter with which you need to come to terms.

We have not come to terms with this question. Let's address the issue right on. The significance of keeping your thoughts in agreement with God's Word is as follows:

Seeing from God's Perspective

Keeping your thoughts in line with God's Word breeds the ability to see from God's perspective. You have to see as God sees and the only way that can happen is by paying attention to God's Word. You may be going through a situation right now, and the world and everyone else may see it from a different perspective. However, for God's Word to be your guarantee, you have to see from God's perspective, through what His Word says about you and the situation through which you are going. It is an absolute fact that it is the Word of God that will keep you in check.

Walking in the Light of God's Word

"The entrance of thy words giveth light; it giveth understanding unto the simple" (Psalms 119:130).

Walking in the light of God's Word, without doubt, implies walking by divine revelation and inspiration. The Psalmist declares and elaborates that walking in the light of God's Word enables us to align with God's Word, "precept upon precept, line upon line," and it is a necessity if you are going to keep your thoughts lined up with God's Word (see Isaiah 28:10). This will happen when the light of God's Word illuminates your understanding, for where there is light, darkness disappears.

Walking in the Spirit

Keeping your thoughts in line with God's Word helps you walk in the Spirit. Apostle Paul declares that we should, *"...Walk in the Spirit and ye shall not fulfil the lust of the flesh"* (see Galatians 5:16). There is no way that you can keep your thoughts on God's Words and walk in the flesh. The flesh always wants to fulfill the cravings of the flesh while the spirit ever intends to satisfy the yearnings of the Spirit. Again, walking in the Spirit does not indicate being mysterious or unnatural, it means to be led by God's Spirit and His Word.

Victory over Sin

"Thy word have I hid in mine heart, that I might not sin against thee" (Psalm 119:11).

The Psalmist helps us understand that when God's Word is concealed in our hearts, it helps keep us away from sinning against God. The sin of any kind breeds separation from God and causes the Word of God to become ineffective in your life. When we are ruled and dominated by sin, we become enemies of God (see Romans 8:7). The Word of God assists in putting our thoughts and actions under control so that our reasoning is not contrary to God and His Word. Aligning our thoughts with God's Word exposes the sin in our hearts, thus, enabling us to deal with it in the light of Scriptures.

HOW TO KEEP YOUR THOUGHTS ALIGNED WITH GOD'S WORD

· ·

Through Meditation

"I will meditate in thy precepts, and have respect unto thy ways. I will delight myself in thy statutes: I will not forget thy word" (Psalms 119:15-16).

Above all else, let your thoughts honor God. God promises that His Word will be a light to our path (see Psalms 119:105), so the more we think upon and meditate on His Word, the brighter our tracks become. Webster's Revised Unabridged Dictionary 1913 defines meditation as "the act of meditating; close or continued thought; the turning or revolving of a subject in the mind; serious contemplation; reflection; musing" and meditate as "to keep the mind in a state of contemplation; to dwell on anything in thought, to think seriously; to muse; to cogitate; to reflect" (see Psalms 19:14 & 1:2) respectively.

Biblical meditation is the practice of pondering, considering, and reflecting on verses of Scripture in total dependence on the Holy Spirit to give a revelation of truth and meaning. It is crucial that you understand that what you meditate gets amplified in your life. Hence, you have to meditate God's Word to keep your thoughts in line with His Word (see 1 Timothy 4:15).

Joshua 1:8 states that *"This book of the law shall not depart out of thy mouth; but thou shalt meditate therein day and night, that thou mayest observe to do according to all that is written therein: for then thou shalt make thy way prosperous, and then thou shalt have good success."* The Psalmist also says, *"Mine eyes prevent the night watches, that I might meditate in thy word"* (Psalms 119:148). This process, I believe, helped David to keep his thoughts aligned with God's Word before and during his reign as King. The importance of meditation on God's Word cannot be overstated as it engenders you to stay focussed and have the right perspective on every aspect of your life.

Through Memorization of Scriptures

"By which also ye are saved, if ye keep in memory what I preached unto you, unless ye have believed in vain" (1 Corinthians 15:2).

Memorizing God's Word assists us in understanding and assimilating God's Word. This is helpful because the unexpected can happen to us in uncertain places and we may not have access to the textual Bible to read or meditate in such times. It is the Scriptures that we have stored up in our mind that we can access in such moment of despair, thus, helping us keep our thoughts in line with His Word without wavering in our trust of God and keeping our mind stayed on Him at all times.

Through the Study of God's Word

The study of God's Word is of the utmost importance. It helps to renew our minds and in turn condition our thoughts to be in line with God's Word. The Scriptures say *"For the word of God is quick, and powerful, and sharper than any two-edged sword, piercing even to the dividing asunder of soul and spirit, and of the joints and marrow, and is a discerner of the thoughts and intents of the heart"* (Hebrews 4:12). The latter part of the text states that God's Word is a *"discerner of the thoughts and intents of the heart."* As we study the Word, it helps to reveal things that we may not know or may have deliberately ignored.

Through Confession of God's Word

As meditation is to think, consider, and to ponder, confession of God's Word is to agree and speak the same things that God's Word has spoken concerning you and your family on a consistent basis regardless of circumstances or situations. Confessing God's Word out of your mouth does something to your thoughts; it enables them to be aligned with God's Word.

Apostle Paul expresses in Romans 10:10, *"For with the heart man believeth unto righteousness, and with the mouth confession is made unto salvation."* The Greek word for *"salvation"* is *Soteria* (Strong's G4991), and it implies the state or act of deliverance, rescue from harm or peril, whether that danger is physical or spiritual. It is imperative to reiterate that a thought life that is not submitted to God and His Word is in danger of destruction. With that said, when we consistently confess God's Word, it affects our thoughts; it makes them whole and aligned to the counsel of God.

Through Prayer

"And it came to pass, that, as he was praying in a certain place, when he ceased, one of his disciples said unto him, Lord, teach us to pray, as John also taught his disciples" (Luke 11:1).

Prayer is a vital key, and it plays a crucial role in our relationship with God. It is the channel through which we communicate with God and God communicates with us. When we consistently approach God and His Word prayerfully, it helps us have an understanding and readjust the alignment of our thoughts with the mind of God.

Jude 1:20 encourages us: *"But ye, beloved, building up yourselves on your most holy faith, praying in the Holy Ghost"* and James 5:16b states that *"The effectual fervent prayer of a righteous man availeth much."* In other words, prayer is useful in its workings in obtaining grace and mercy as we approach the throne of grace to find help in the time of need and turn around any situation (see Hebrews 4:16).

Through Guarding Your Heart

"Keep thy heart with all diligence; for out of it are the issues of life" (Proverbs 4:23).

Guarding your mind takes discipline and diligence. Satan's objective is to get you to receive negative thoughts, and then speak and act on them. Once you take action on something he has suggested, you activate a negative cycle in your life. This is where your resolve must be initiated. Second Corinthians 10:5 says, *"Casting down imaginations, and every high thing that exalteth itself against the knowledge of God, and bringing into captivity every thought to the obedience of Christ;"* God isn't going to defend your mind for you; it's your responsibility. With the Word of God in your mouth and your heart, you can defeat the enemy's suggestions every time.

Our Thoughts Are Captives of the Lord

Apostle Paul in his letter to the Church in Corinth says, *"For it is written, I will destroy the wisdom of the wise, and will bring to nothing the understanding of the prudent"* (2 Corinthians 1:19). The wisdom and thoughts of men resist the knowledge of God's Word. Therefore, to keep our thoughts aligned with God's Word, we must have a personal responsibility to bring every thought (that is, the intent of the mind or will) into captivity to the obedience to Christ, submitting and to obeying God's Word.

BENEFITS OF ALIGNING YOUR THOUGHTS WITH GOD'S WORD

· ·

Established Thoughts

Proverbs 16:3 declares, *"Commit thy works unto the LORD, and thy thoughts shall be established."* It is desirable to have our thoughts established. Consequently, as you commit your thoughts to the Lord, the object of your thoughts will be established so you will not be tossed back and forth. When a man is unstable in the realm of his thoughts, he will be unstable in all of his ways. This is one of the most significant benefits of keeping your thinking aligned with God's Word.

Answered Prayers

You have answers to your prayers when you keep your thoughts aligned with God's Word. It is imperative that you understand this because negative thoughts sabotage your prayers. It is not uncommon to find that most Christians after they have prayed negate their prayers with negative thinking and speaking. For instance, you have prayed and believed God for healing, and instead of aligning your thoughts with God's Word, you allow negative thoughts to inundate your mind, making the Word of God seem to be of no effect.

Abundant Life

"The thief cometh not, but for to steal, and to kill, and to destroy: I am come that they might have life, and that they might have it more abundantly" (John 10:10)

This is victorious living in all areas. Aligning our thoughts with God's Word helps us to think like God and not just like ordinary men. It is, therefore, appropriate to say that to the degree that my thoughts are aligned with God's Word is to the same degree I will enjoy abundant life. Now, that may sound outrageous to some of you, but hear me out first.

There are two words I would like to consider – *"abundant"* and *"life."* First, let us examine the Greek word for *"abundant,"* which is *Perissós* (Strong's G4053). It implies, "superabundant (in quantity) or superior (in quality), excessive, advantage, exceedingly, very highly; and beyond measure." Secondly, "Life" is *Zōé* (Strong's G2222) in Greek and it means "that which makes God; the God-kind of life." Now, child of God, this is the kind of life that can only be enjoyed as you keep your thoughts in check by adhering to God's Word.

Walking in Perfect Peace

Perfect peace is given only to those whose minds and hearts are fixed on God and His eternal Word. Isaiah, the Prophet, says, *"Thou wilt keep him in perfect peace, whose mind is stayed on thee: because he trusteth in thee"* (Isaiah 26:3). What is this peace? It is an inner sense of contentment and quietness, regardless of life's circumstances. The person whose thoughts are aligned and dependent on God's Word in times of trouble will experience this inner sense of contentment and quietness regardless of what they may be experiencing in their lives.

Sometimes you may not know how to deal with a situation at hand, but because your mind stays on God and His Word, your heart is reassured by the peace of God that passes all human understanding. The Psalmist observes that *"Great peace have they which love thy law: and nothing shall offend them"* (Psalms 119:165). As you align your thoughts with God's Word, you will start loving God's law, which engenders peace that passes all understanding.

Guidance

The Word of God is our chart and compass; it serves as our guidebook for our pilgrimage here on earth. In Proverbs 3:5-6, the Bible says, *Trust in the Lord with all thine heart; and lean not unto thine own understanding. In all thy ways acknowledge him, and he shall direct thy paths.* As you can imagine, your everyday life is full of decisions, and if you are going to make the right ones that will bring God glory and benefit others and yourself, you will continually be in need of God's comprehensive guidance.

In his letter to Timothy Apostle Paul writes, *"All scripture is given by inspiration of God, and is profitable for doctrine, for reproof, for correction, for instruction in righteousness: That the man of God may be perfect, thoroughly furnished unto all good works"* (2 Timothy 3:16-17). As you align your thoughts with God's Word, you start submitting to the counsel of God. There are fantastic benefits in aligning your thoughts with God's Word.

Cleanses

Psalms 119:9 declares, *"Wherewithal shall a young man cleanse his way? by taking heed thereto according to thy word."* The cleansing effect of the Word of God in our lives cannot be overemphasized. When you are first born again, your spirit man is born again. The human mind and its desires are still in its fallen condition at this time. In Romans 12:2 we are told: *"...be not conformed to this world: but be ye transformed by the renewing of your mind, that ye may prove what is that good, and acceptable, and perfect, will of God."* As a result of studying God's Word and aligning our thoughts with it, we begin to experience our minds being renewed and our thoughts gradually coming into alignment with the Word of God.

There are grave consequences of not keeping our thoughts on God's Word. This is one area where the enemy always strives to keep the child of God in captivity because he knows that once our thoughts are not in line with God's Word, we are paralyzed, unable to do much, and so we will not be a threat to his kingdom. Here are some consequences that can occur as a result of not keeping your thoughts in line with God's Word:

1. A mind that is the Devil's playground

2. Inability to discern and walk in the will of God
3. Leaning on your understanding and not God's
4. Doubt and unbelief
5. Hindrances to prayer
6. A mind that is a haven for impure thoughts

Let's move on to the next chapter with your determination to keep your thoughts aligned with God's Word because your thoughts are of the utmost importance in the ultimate fulfillment of your destiny, so begin now by learning to keep your thoughts aligned to God's Word daily. Yes, you can!

CHAPTER 10

THE WILDERNESS LIFE OF THE BELIEVER

"Now all these things happened to them for examples, and they are written for our admonition, upon whom the ends of the ages have come" (1 Corinthians 10:11 NJKV).

It is imperative that we examine how the children of Israel conducted themselves as they were faced with adverse conditions, as they were led from the land of bondage through the wilderness to the land of promise. We will also examine their actions during the journey and how this affected their relationship with God and His established leadership, Moses. The Scripture declares that these things happened and are written for our admonition, for as we examine the Bible's content, the Holy Spirit will illuminate, help us understand, and apply the lessons learned to our daily lives.

Now when a sinner is delivered from the bondage of sin and death by the power of God, they are led by the Spirit of God in their Christian walk and experiences, and this leading of the Holy Spirit prepares them for the Promised Land - the kingdom of God promised to those who are born again. Jesus answered, in response to Nicodemus' question, *"Verily, verily, I say unto thee, 'Except a man be born of water and the Spirit, he cannot enter into the kingdom of God'"* (John 3:5). Nicodemus, a ruler of the Jews who came to Jesus by night, did not understand the meaning of what he had said in the previous verse, as a consequence, the Lord Jesus explained to him the significance of what He meant by telling him that the birth He spoke about was not natural, but spiritual. That is, to be born of the water which signifies the Word of God and the Spirit.

To examine all that happened to the Israelites is advantageous as they are landmark experiences, which we as believers should learn from on our journey to our Promised Land as we experience the same limitations and potentially react just as they did during their travels through the wilderness.

Two prominent features that characterized their journey through the wilderness were the presence of:

1. The pillar of cloud by day
2. The pillar of fire by night

These represent the presence of the Holy Spirit to guide them day and night throughout their journey. They also symbolize the same presence with us today as our guide through our wilderness leading into our promise land. It is evident today that most Christian believers, like the majority of the children of Israel, wandered or are still wandering in their spiritual wilderness for not acknowledging the presence of the Holy Spirit and ignoring God's Word. This has cut them off from experiencing the promises of God.

As New Testament believers, we can identify with the fear, thirst, hunger, doubt, despair, and idol worship, among other distractions the children of Israel had while on their journey through the wilderness.

FEAR

....

"And when Pharaoh drew nigh, the children of Israel lifted up their eyes, and, behold, the Egyptians marched after them; and they were sore afraid: and the children of Israel cried out unto the LORD. And they said unto Moses, 'Because there were no graves in Egypt, hast thou taken us away to die in the wilderness? wherefore hast thou dealt thus with us, to carry us forth out of Egypt? Is not this the word that we did tell thee in Egypt, saying, "Let us alone, that we may serve the Egyptians?" For it had been better for us to serve the Egyptians, than that we should die in the wilderness.' And Moses said unto the people, 'Fear ye not, stand still, and see the salvation of the LORD, which he will shew to you today: for the Egyptians whom ye have seen to day, ye shall see them again no more for ever. The LORD shall fight for you, and ye shall hold your peace'" (Exodus 14:10-14).

The children of Israel became apprehensive, knowing that Pharaoh and his armies marched right behind them and they could not advance because the Red Sea was ahead of them. This situation arises now and then in our lives' journey. Knowing what God's Word declares and accepting the guidance it offers is critical. We would have thought that having seen the wonders that God displayed in the land of Egypt, the children of Israel would have trusted God entirely for protection and deliverance and would not have allowed themselves to be distracted.

It is evident that we, as believers today, tend to fear and doubt God and His Word when Satan and his cohorts launch attacks against our lives. False evidence appearing real (FEAR) has also deprived quite a number of us of the fulfillment of God's promises in our walk with the Lord. Though God has delivered us from the bondage of sin and death, some of us are still hanging on the threshold of the Promised Land because of the enslavement of fear.

The Scripture declares, *"For God hath not given us the spirit of fear; but of power, and of love, and of a sound mind"* (2 Timothy 1:7). We have not been given the spirit of fear; therefore, if it is not from God from whom does it originate? Of course, it is from the devil. Do not be ignorant of the devil's devices. Get ahold of God's Word; resist the spirit of fear, and it will flee. Fear incarcerates its victim and immobilizes them in their pursuit of God. It will sabotage your aspirations and efforts as you pursue your God-given destiny. You must not allow this to happen. The presence of fear in any man's life is indicative of the absence of light and the Word of God. Hence, when fear shows its ugly head, engage God's Word.

THIRST

. . . .

"So Moses brought Israel from the Red Sea, and they went out into the wilderness of Shur; and they went three days in the wilderness, and found no water. And when they came to Marah, they could not drink of the waters of Marah, for they were bitter: therefore the name of it was called Marah. And the people murmured against Moses, saying, 'What shall we drink?' And he cried unto the LORD; and the LORD shewed him a tree, which when he had cast into the waters, the waters were made sweet: there he made for them a statute and an ordinance, and there he proved them, And said, 'If thou wilt diligently hearken to the voice of the LORD thy God, and wilt do that which is right in his sight, and wilt give ear to his commandments, and keep all his statutes, I will put none of these diseases upon thee, which I have brought upon the Egyptians: for I am the LORD that healeth thee.' And they came to Elim, where were twelve wells

of water, and threescore and ten palm trees: and they encamped there by the waters" (Exodus 15:22-27).

In the above passage, we see that as the children of Israel journeyed, they became thirsty, and when they finally found water, it was bitter, which of course rendered it unsuitable for drinking. As usual, they began to murmur and complain; a situation comparable to many Christians as we go through life and become spiritually exhausted and thirsty for a spiritual drink. As that water was made suitable for the children of Israel to drink, today God is still able to do the same for us. For Jesus Christ is the same yesterday and today and forever (Hebrews 13:8). Nevertheless, we must stay focused on God and His Word.

In John 7:37-38, Jesus Christ declares, "If any man thirst, let him come to me, and drink" and "out of his belly shall flow rivers of living water." In the account of Jesus with the Samaritan woman in (John 4:14), it says, *"But whosoever drinketh of the water that I shall give him shall never thirst; but the water that I shall give him shall be in him a well of water springing up into everlasting life."* It was evident that this woman was physically and spiritually exhausted from her life situation and needed help. According to the words of Jesus, all she was required to do was to "Ho, every one that thirsteth, come ye to the waters" (see Isaiah 55:1).

Like the Samaritan women, we are overwhelmed with life situations, although our conditions may not be as dramatic as hers. However, in some ways, we are subjected to disappointments, failures, and frustrations that leave us physically and spiritually exhausted just like what this Samaritan woman might have experienced. Blessed be God forever, for we have access to the same life-transforming rivers of living waters that can quench our thirst and reinvigorate us if only we can believe.

COMPLAINING

. . . .

The scriptural account in (Exodus 16:1-21) lets us understand how the children of Israel ran out of food and again began to grumble and complain against God; His servants had forgotten how the Lord God had led and kept them up to that point. Can we honestly relate to this today as children of God? Of course, yes. We are often found grumbling and complaining about one thing or the other instead of thanking God for what He has done and His benefits toward us, believing His word and praying to Him in faith to do the same again and again. *"Bless the LORD, O my soul: and all that is within me, bless his holy name. Bless the LORD, O my soul, and forget not all his benefits: Who forgiveth all thine iniquities; who healeth all thy diseases"* (Psalms 103:1-3).

We need to understand that murmuring and grumbling are symptoms of a starved soul. Indications of this could be that our prayer time with the Lord has been exchanged for unimportant adventures or curtailed and Bible study neglected. These impediments result in murmuring and grumbling. Apostle Paul admonishes us in Philippians 2:14 that we should "Do all things without murmuring or disputes:" You must understand that unwarranted expression of discontentment and unnecessary argument grieve God and thus, can limit the efficacy of God's Word in your life. Therefore, quit murmuring and focus on God and His Word as the final arbiter in your life.

HUNGER

. . . .

As the children of Israel journeyed, they became hungry and completely forgot how God on several occasions met their needs supernaturally. Having forgotten, they started complaining and murmuring about God and His servants, Moses and Aaron. They accused them of bringing the children of Isreal to the wilderness to kill them with hunger. Our God is merciful and full of compassion, so regardless of their disobedience and complaints, He gave them manna, bread from Heaven (see Exodus 16:1-21).

Born-again believers who hunger because of unprecedented journeys that they have taken during their Christian wilderness experiences need not expect manna to fall from Heaven as true manna has already come in the person of Jesus Christ. The Bible declares in John 6:35 that *"And Jesus said unto them, I am the bread of life: he that cometh to me shall never hunger; and he that believeth on me shall never thirst."* We become spiritually exhausted and hungry because we often starve our spirit man of the precious Word of God, which the Apostle Peter refers to in 1 Peter 2:2, *"As newborn babes, desire the sincere milk of the word, that ye may grow thereby."*

In our spiritual walk and daily life experiences as we journey through the wilderness to the Promised Land, we need to feed on God's Word for sustenance, strength, and direction. Job elucidates in Job 23:12: *"Neither have I gone back from the commandment of his lips; I have esteemed the words of his mouth more than my necessary food."* Jeremiah 15:16 also says, *"Thy words were found, and I did eat them; and thy word was unto me the joy and rejoicing of mine heart: for I am called by thy name, O LORD God of hosts."* Both Job and Jeremiah expressed the value and significance of feeding on God's Word and how they have made it a part of their lives to treasure up God's Word.

We are all susceptible to going through the wilderness at one point in our lives' journey, remember that the Word of God is your ultimate guarantee; so, endeavor to feed and nourish yourself on it consistently.

DOUBT AND DESPAIR

Another experience that characterized the journey of the Israelites on their way through the wilderness was doubt and despair. James explicitly declares in James 1:8: *"A double minded man is unstable in all his ways."* Uncertainty leads to conflicts within us as we become double-minded and unstable in our ways. Frequently, in our wilderness experiences, we are confronted with all kinds of challenges that are humanly impossible to resolve, and as a result, we are inclined to doubt God's Word and question His integrity and His ability to do what He said He would do.

The people demonstrated outright disobedience and faithlessness; remember, without faith, no man can please God (see Hebrews 11:6). It is of the utmost importance to understand that despite our wilderness experience, the perpetual barrage of things coming at us, we must be resolved in rejecting doubt and assert confidence in God's Word as our ultimate guarantee in all matters of life. Doubt and unbelief cut us off from the spiritual life flow and the manifestation of the power of God in our lives (see Mark 6:5-6). Don't limit God's power working in your circumstances through doubt and unbelief.

IDOL WORSHIP

. . . .

Exodus 32:1-32 shows us one of the most grievous errors the children of Israel got themselves into during their wilderness experience. Their idol worship was an outright rebellion against God, which is true of anyone who is involved in any form of idol worship. You may not necessarily worship graven images today, but I submit to you that anything or anyone that takes preeminence in your life above God is an idol. Examples include careers, ambitions, husbands, or wives.

As you continue to grow to make God's Word your guarantee, you will overcome the challenges you will face in your wilderness journey toward your Promised Land. Stay the course!

CHAPTER 11

THE BATTLE OF CONTAINMENT

"'Sing, O barren, thou that didst not bear; break forth into singing, and cry aloud, thou that didst not travail with child: for more are the children of the desolate than the children of the married wife,' saith the LORD. 'Enlarge the place of thy tent, and let them stretch forth the curtains of thine habitations: spare not, lengthen thy cords, and strengthen thy stakes; For thou shalt break forth on the right hand and on the left; and thy seed shall inherit the Gentiles, and make the desolate cities to be inhabited'" (Isaiah 54:1-3).

WHAT IS THE BATTLE OF CONTAINMENT?

. . . .

M erriam-Webster Dictionary defines containment as "the act, process, or means of keeping something within limits." Therefore, containment means, "to restrain or contain someone within certain fixed limits, to hold back something from its full expression, or to hold back something from manifesting its full capacity and capabilities."

Consequently, these battles of containment are the wiles of the enemy devised to suppress, control, manipulate or restrain us, that is, contain us within certain fixed limits in any way possible and hinder us from becoming what Jehovah God has ordained for us to become.

The woman with the issue of blood was contained by the affliction and kept in bondage for twelve years (see Mark 5:25-34). Another woman was afflicted and held in bondage for eighteen years (see Luke 13:16). Another man was sick of the palsy, and his friends brought him to Jesus. They were undeterred by the flood of people around Jesus, went up on the roof, and lowered the sick man at His feet (see Mark 2:1-4). The list continues. Today, many are subjected to similar battles of containment one way or the other. To break free from any containment, we need to engage the power of the Word of God and come against the onslaught of the enemy in all areas of life.

Apostle Paul admonishes us in Ephesians 6:11 to *"Put on the whole armor of God, that ye may be able to stand against the wiles of the devil."* The Greek word for *"wiles"* is *Methodeia* (Strong's G3180), which denotes craftiness, deceit, cunning arts, trickery, or deception practiced for ensnaring. Apostle Paul here reveals that the purpose for putting on the whole armor of God is to enable you to stand against; that is, to take a position in front of and oppose all the crafts, deceits, and cunning devices of the enemy, which he employs against us in this battle of containment. The devil can keep you contained in any way possible to achieve his goals.

The Hebrew word for *"enlarge"* is *Râchab* (Strong's H7337), meaning "to broaden, to make large, make room and make wide open," while the Hebrew word for *"break forth"* is *Pârats* (Strong's H6555), which means to 'break out; break forth; breakthrough; burst; increase, disperse and scatter." This implies that you must breakthrough every battle of containment in any area of your life and allow God to work in your life. It is imperative that you understand that the battle of containment is an issue that is worth taking into consideration as it affects the Body of Christ a great deal.

The accuser of the brethren, the devil, has continuously waged a battle of containment against us as individuals, families, and as a Church, hindering most people from fulfilling their God-given destinies and possessing the promises of God's Word. This war of containment tries to keep us in Egypt when the Promised Land awaits us.

The devil seems to be successful at his schemes primarily because of your ignorance of God's Word. The enemy may get you so occupied in achieving this goal or that goal without you stepping into the things that God has ordained for you. Neither is he interested in your going to the Church or engaging in any religious activities or falling under the power of God as long as you are indifferent, unwilling to change and lukewarm toward the things of God and His kingdom.

This battle of containment is raging and fought in the form of financial, health, or family strongholds, imaginations, and things such as human ideologies try to exalt themselves above and against the knowledge of God and His Word in your life, thus, keeping you as you are.

THE SWORD OF THE SPIRIT

· ·

"Put on the whole armor of God that ye may be able to stand against the wiles of the devil. For we wrestle not against flesh and blood, but against principalities, against powers, against the rulers of the darkness of this world, against spiritual wickedness in high places. Wherefore take unto you the whole armor of God that ye may be able to withstand in the evil day, and having done all, to stand. Stand therefore, having your loins girt about with truth, and having on the breastplate of righteousness; And your feet shod with the preparation of the gospel of peace; Above all,

> *taking the shield of faith, wherewith ye shall be able*
> *to quench all the fiery darts of the wicked. And take*
> *the helmet of salvation, and the sword of the Spirit,*
> *which is the Word of God:"* (Ephesians 6:11-17).

There are five essential postures for the believer to assume to be effective and victorious in the battle of containment that the enemy wages. It is vital to know that this battle is an active one and not passive like most Christians consider it to be. The postures are as follows:

- to stand against, which means to stand in front of and oppose (Verse 11)
- to wrestle, which means to engage actively in a one-on-one battle (Verse 12)
- to withstand, which indicates resistance; it also means to be firm and unmovable in encountering opposition (Verse 13)
- to stand, which means to be found standing after an active battle (Verse 13
- stand, therefore, which means to take your stand for the next fight (Verse 14)

The Word of God is the sword of the Spirit, a very vital and a useful tool in the believer's life. It is imperative to understand the assailant, to withstand the enemy's onslaughts and maneuvers, for that is when we recognize the nature and effectiveness of our armor. Erroneously, we have maintained that the sword of the Spirit is the sword of the Holy Spirit. Understand that when Apostle Paul enumerated the whole amour of God, his reference was to man, of which he used phrases like you, ye, your, or we, indicating that it is our responsibility to appropriate the whole armor of God including the sword of the Spirit, which is God's Word.

We have assumed the sword of the Spirit to mean the sword of the Holy Spirit. As a result of this inaccurate assumption, we have become spectators rather than participators, waiting on the Holy Spirit to use the sword of our spirit (the Word of God), which is intended for our use. When you do not use the sword, you allow the assailant to get away with their assault on you, your family, finances, ministry, business, and any other aspect of your life to which he has access. Child of God, it is an unimaginable tragedy to neglect the most valuable, offensive weapon that can arrest and frustrate every attack of the enemy.

Understand that the Word of God is the sword of your spirit man which you wield against every onslaught of the enemy and it is used to pull down every stronghold in your life. To be effective, God's Word must have become flesh in you that is allowing God's Word to dwell and permeate every fiber of your being and be quickened by the Holy Spirit when the need arises.

TAKING THE SWORD OF THE SPIRIT

. . . .

"Above all, taking the shield of faith, wherewith ye shall be able to quench all the fiery darts of the wicked. And take the helmet of salvation, and the sword of the Spirit, which is the Word of God:" (Ephesians 6:16-17).

The Scripture admonishes us to take the sword of the Spirit, but the question is how do you do that? It is evident that most Christians tend to search through a concordance or Bible commentaries in times of adversity for that magical word that is supposed to be the sword of the Spirit to enable them to assault the devil and his cohorts. However, this is a very wrong way of taking the sword of the Spirit and explains why most of us have not been able to invade the assailant and his cohorts and see victory repeatedly in our walk with God and our profession of faith.

In 1 Timothy 4:13, Apostle Paul instructs his son in the faith, Timothy, saying, *"Till I come, give attendance to reading, to exhortation, to doctrine"* and recapitulates in 2 Timothy 2:15 that Timothy should *"Study to shew thyself approved unto God, a workman that needeth not to be ashamed, rightly dividing the word of truth.*" This indicates that taking the sword of the Spirit entails *giving attention* to reading, exhortation, doctrine, studying, meditating, memorizing, and storing up God's Word in our spirit man, which will eventually renew our minds so that we do not conform to this world.

Doing this on a consistent basis, long before the adversary and his cohorts show up, will put us in a better position to exercise the sword of the Spirit. When the enemy comes with his onslaught, the Word of God that you have studied, meditated, and memorized will rise from the inside of you, becoming a sword with which you can effectively engage in spiritual warfare.

UNDERSTANDING THE
NATURE OF THE WAR

. . . .

"Lest Satan should get an advantage of us: for we are not ignorant of his devices" (2 Corinthians 2:11).

"So that Satan will not outsmart us. For we are familiar with his evil schemes" (New Living Translation, 2 Corinthians 2:11).

One of the contributing factors to why many Christians are not walking in daily victory is the fact that they do not understand the nature of the war they are engaged in every now and again. You must realize that ignorance of the nature of the war and the enemy's evil schemes will enable him to outwit you in the battle, which can result in unbearable suffering. For this reason, it is imperative to understand the nature of the war in which you are engaged. For example, the nature of the war on our finances, families, businesses, and our ministries has to be understood to appropriately deploy the weapons that God has given us to become winners. It is imperative to know that knowledge is a proper application of what you understand. Therefore, if you must overcome, as admonished by Scripture, you ought not to be ignorant of the devil's devices.

Here, Apostle Paul vividly reveals to the Church the nature of the war in the following Scriptural passages: *"For we wrestle not against flesh and blood, but against principalities, against powers, against the rulers of the darkness of this world, against spiritual wickedness in high places"* and *"For though we walk in the flesh, we do not war after the flesh: (For the weapons of our warfare are not carnal, but mighty through God to the pulling down of strongholds;"* (Ephesians 6:12 and 2 Corinthians 10:3-4) respectively.

The Scriptures above clearly elucidate that the warfare and the arms with which we engage in this battle are not carnal but spiritual. Consequently, tragedy will be inevitable if we participate in the war with carnal weapons as if it were in the physical. This is the dilemma of most believers, for humans tend to employ physical weapons in spiritual warfare. Consequently, they become victims rather than victors.

ALL THINGS WORK TOGETHER FOR GOOD

· ·

"And we know that all things work together for good to them that love God, to them who are the called according to his purpose" (Romans 8:28).

The battle of containment is an ongoing assault of the enemy waged against us to stifle our God-given potential to fulfill our purpose and destiny. On close examination of God's Word, it is evident that the battle of containment is against the purpose for which you were created.

God called Abraham to a land that He would show him. He established His covenant with him and promised to bless all families of the earth through him (see Genesis 12:1-2). In all of that, the devil could not stop him, or cause him to retrogress, but decided to contain him in his relationship with his wife, in that they could not have a child. Abraham eventually had a son with the Egyptian handmaid, a situation that became a matter of alternative, a battle of containment (see Genesis 16:1-6). In spite of the Word of promise, Abraham took control of the situation into his own hands instead of allowing God to take the absolute control and perfect all that He had promised.

Abraham was not ignorant of the devil's devices but learned the consequences of not listening to God's Word and went on to obtain his victory, standing on God's Word, which was his guarantee to the fulfillment of every promise. Regardless of what we may go through in life, we can rest assured that all things work together for good for those that love the Lord and we must learn to hold on tenaciously to God's Word in all situations, knowing that God's Word is our guarantee. Abraham did, and when you do, you will experience the promises of God come to fruition in your own life.

DREAMS COME TRUE

. . . .

"And Joseph dreamed a dream, and he told it his brethren: and they hated him yet the more" (Genesis 37:5).

God gave Joseph a dream, and in that dream, He showed Joseph the purpose for which he was born. The dream held the potential for a successful life, blessings, and prosperity for others. There is a God-given dream for everyone to fulfill on the face of the earth, which should ultimately culminate in successful lives, blessings, and prosperity for others. However, this is often not the outcome because of the battle of containment, for as you immediately discover your dream and what God's Word declares concerning you, the enemy tries to sabotage your dream and contain you in whatever way possible.

Joseph's brothers sold him into slavery, and Potiphar's wife attempted sexual pervasion with him and lied against him because of his refusal to yield to her persuasions. She also had him imprisoned, and his friends forgot him in prison. These were schemes to inhibit him from experiencing the fulfillment of his God-given dream. However, he held on to God's Word. God ultimately rewarded the outcome of Joseph's faithfulness tremendously. By the hand of God, Joseph was elevated from the prison to the palace; and a place of prominence next to Pharoah of Egpyt (see Genesis 41:1-57). In so many aspects, the Church today is attacked with containment, in our gifts, dreams, finances, marriages, relationships, and ministries individually and collectively as a people.

It has become imperative to emphasize that even when a visionary's dream or purpose is subjected to adverse conditions, know that as long as that dream or vision is born of God, it has the inherent potency to come to fruition and maturation even when it is not visible to the ordinary eye. Know beyond a shadow of a doubt that the dream-giver is still in control of the situation and His Word will come to pass in your life in due season. Glory be to God.

> *"The thief cometh not, but for to steal, and to kill, and to destroy: I am come that they might have life, and that they might have it more abundantly"* (John 10:10)

The devil is a thief who comes to steal, kill, and to destroy, but he recognizes that he cannot stop or push you out of your purpose, so he schemes to contain you, making you comfortable with your status in life without progression. So many Christians all over the world, although looking and acting comfortable, are contained by the devil. The Word of God says, *"And from the days of John the Baptist until now the kingdom of heaven suffereth violence, and the violent take it by force"* (Matthew 11:12). This implies that a battle is waged violently against us, and it will demand persistent believers to take and possess what is rightfully theirs, standing upon the Word of God. It is imperative to break out of this cocoon of containment violently.

CHAPTER 12

WHOSE REPORT WILL YOU BELIEVE?

"Behold, the LORD thy God hath set the land before thee: go up and possess it, as the LORD God of thy fathers hath said unto thee; 'fear not, neither be discouraged. And ye came near unto me every one of you, and said, "We will send men before us, and they shall search us out the land, and bring us word by what way we must go up, and into what cities we shall come"' (Deuteronomy 1:21-22).

In the above passages, we notice that the children of Israel resolved in their minds to request that spies be sent to search out the land, which the Lord had previously promised to give them for their possession. The dialogue, as well as the action undertaken by the children of Israel, was an indication that they lacked the knowledge and the understanding of the counsel of God, which ultimately was unbelief in God's Word. This, of course, led to planning and acting on their initiative. Child of God, whenever you do not understand the counsel and mind of God, whatever you do becomes an alternative to what God had already promised you. Unbelief, therefore, is not acknowledging and acting on God's

Word. Furthermore, unbelief is going your way, choosing what you see as popular and preferred by the majority at the expense of God's Word.

Moses went to God with the demands of the children of Israel not knowing the profundity of unbelief embedded in their hearts. But God who weighs the thoughts and intents of man's heart gave them up to their reprobate minds to do those things that they appraised convenient and pleasing to themselves. This is true and very much the situation today in the lives of many sincere children of God. We often don't take God at His Word or believe His promises for us. Rather, we choose to believe man's report and what circumstances dictate, which is a reflection of our unbelief and rebellion against God.

On close examination of the situation the Israelites faced, we find conclusive evidence that shows that unbelief was embedded in their hearts:

- *Search out the land*: It was God's covenant promise to bring the children of Israel to the land of promise. God had already searched out the land, which flowed with milk and honey, but they chose to believe the reports of the spies, and walk by sight and not by faith in God's report.
- *Bring us a word*: From the Scriptural passages above, we discover that God had previously spoken His Word to them, but the children of Israel still desired a word from man irrespective of God's Word. This indicates that they had more confidence in the words of men than God's.
- *The way we must go*: God already made the provision, therefore, seeking out the way for themselves was a demonstration that they lacked confidence in His directions and guidance, despite the experiences they encountered when God brought them out of the land of bondage: such as the pillar of cloud and fire, being fed with manna, parting the Red Sea, and the sweetening of bitter water at Mara, etc...

- *What cities we shall come:* God had already chosen the city. To them, though, the city selected by the spies was most appropriate. This is reminiscent of the fact that they had no confidence in God's judgment.

The Scriptures declare in Numbers 13: 1-2, *"And the Lord spake unto Moses, saying, 'Send thou men, that they may search the land of Canaan, which I give unto the children of Israel: of every tribe of their fathers shall ye send a man, everyone a ruler among them.'"* Here, we see Moses sending out men to explore the land of Canaan at the command of God. God promised the children of Israel that He was going to bring them into a land that flowed with milk and honey. One would think that God meant what He said and said what He meant, without the help of spies.

Notwithstanding, the children of Israel did not have such an evaluation of the issue concerning the above text, but requested and inclined themselves to sending spies into the land before stepping in to occupy the land. Understand that it was not God's initiative neither was it Moses' to send spies into the land but the initiative of the people of Israel.

It is imperative to know that different people react in different ways when subjected to the same situations or circumstances. However, these reactions should be based on the knowledge of God's Word possessed. For instance, the ten other men that brought the evil report with Joshua and Caleb were given the same instructions and subjected to the same situation. They all saw the same things, the same people, and spied the same land, but the perceptions and reactions of the ten men were entirely different from those of Joshua and Caleb.

On the other hand, the multitude that remained at home believed the evil report because their mindset was that the majority was right even though what they said was not aligned with God's Word, which of course was not always the case. This is also apparently seen today in our individual and collective lives as children of God. What could be responsible for this glaring difference between these men?

- They both *heard* God's report, but Joshua and Caleb *believed* God's report.
- The ten spies saw themselves in the perspective of the prevailing circumstance; however, Joshua and Caleb saw themselves from the perspective of God's report (His Word).
- Joshua and Caleb kept God's report in their hearts.
- Joshua and Caleb meditated God's report (God's Word).
- God's Word was Joshua and Caleb's measuring standard no matter the circumstance.

GOD'S REPORT VERSUS MAN'S REPORT

· ·

"Who hath believed our report? and to whom is the arm of the LORD revealed?" (Isaiah 53:1)

"Who has believed our message? To whom has the LORD revealed his powerful arm?" (New Living Translation, Isaiah 53:1)

Whose report will you believe? The New Living Translation puts it thus: "Who has believed our message?" To whom will the LORD reveal His powerful arm? Whose message will you believe: God's or man's, God's Word or your circumstance? Whose and what report or message you believe will ultimately determine whose arm (strength and power) will be revealed or manifested on your behalf. You can find solace in God's Word, knowing that *"With men it is impossible, but not with God: for with God all things are possible"* (Mark 10:27). Hence, if you believe the report of the Lord, the arm of the Lord, which is the awesome and saving power of God, His authority, His protection, His mercy, and His forgiveness will be activated and manifested on your behalf.

Whatever you are going through or your condition in life, whether you're sick, oppressed, tormented, or impoverished, do not believe the reports of the doctors or man's opinion and judgment of the situation. Believe and tenaciously hold onto God's report and evaluation of the situation. God's report is the final arbiter for whatever you are going through. The report of the Lord says you are healed, delivered, set free, and prosperous. Be bold to align yourself with God's report by declaring with your mouth and believing in your heart what your mouth confesses.

GOD'S REPORT

God's report is His Word, will, and purpose. In the events of life, irrespective of the situations or circumstances that occur, what God says is His report, and it will ultimately stand unaltered and efficacious if believed and heeded. The Scripture declares, *"'I know the thoughts that I think toward you,' saith the LORD, 'thoughts of peace, and not of evil, to give you an expected end'"* (Jeremiah 29:11). The New Living Translation puts it thus, *"For I know the plans I have for you,' says the LORD. 'They are plans for good and not for disaster, to give you a future and a hope.'"* This is God's report for you, your family, and everything that concerns you. It is imperative to know and be engrossed in the fact that God's report is not circumstantial; neither does it depend on what we experience or not. His Word must be tenaciously held in order to experience the fulfillment of God's promises as stated in His Word.

MAN'S REPORT

Man's report is his word, will, and personal agendas. Man's report is based on what he can see, feel, and touch. It is the sophisticated thought pattern, opinion, and reasoning of man, which is void of the complete counsel of God's Word. Numbers 13:32 says, *"And they brought up an evil report of the land which they had searched unto the children of Israel, saying, 'The land, through which we have gone to search it, is a land that eateth up the inhabitants thereof'; and all the people that we saw in it are men of a great stature."* The Scripture identifies these as evil reports no matter how reasonable they are. Why are they called "evil"? Because the Word of God is His will, so if your thought patterns and reasoning are not lined up with the Word of God, they do not conform to His will and so are termed "evil."

WALK BY FAITH AND NOT BY SIGHT

"(For we walk by faith, not by sight:)" (2 Corinthians 5:7).

"For we walk by faith (we regulate our lives and conduct ourselves by our conviction or belief respecting man's relationship to God and divine things, with trust and holy fervor; thus we walk) not by sight or appearance." (Amplified Bible Classic Edition, 2 Corinthians 5:7)

"So shall my word be that goeth forth out of my mouth: it shall not return unto me void, but shall accomplish that which I please, and it shall prosper in the thing whereto I sent it" (Isaiah 55: 11)

"It is the same with my word. I send it out, and it always produces fruit. It will accomplish all I want it to, and it will prosper everywhere I send it" (New Living Translation, Isaiah 55:11).

The Greek word for *"walk"* is *Peripateo* (Strong's G4043), meaning "to regulate one's life" or "to conduct one's self." The Greek word for *"sight"* is *Eidos* (Strong's G1491), meaning that which strikes the eyes, that which is exposed to view or external appearance. Not walking by sight simply means we are not to conduct the affairs of our lives based on what we see with the eyes in the natural, instead, we are to conduct ourselves based on the infallible Word of God and that is what it means to walk by faith.

The vision that faith embraces is more tangible than the mere vision of the eyes. Faith is the drive behind your walk or conduct, the instrument by which you are guided, the chief agent through which you aspire to fulfill your God-given destiny. Apostle Paul elucidates that only when using faith can one expect to live a fulfilling life for by faith the just shall live (see Hebrews 10:38).

If faith sees things that the eyes do not see, then it is considered that faith is in sharper focus. It is evident, therefore, that the evidence faith produces based on the Word of God is always authentic and decisive. Whenever any conflict arises between the claims of faith and those of sight, faith must ever be declared victorious in matters of life for no man can please God without faith (see Hebrews 11:6).

Here lies the choice we all must make. Which will dominate, *faith* or *sight*? If it is *sight*, then your soul will remain earth-bound, never able to escape the imprisonment of natural law or the limitations of this worldly sphere. However, if it is faith, then access will be given to you into the holiest, into the glorious presence of God, where the only restriction is the boundary of His almost limitless promise.

The Scripture admonishes us to walk by faith as opposed to walking by sight. We understand that faith comes as a result of God's Word heard and received; therefore, walking by faith is walking by the Word of God. It suffices to say that we ought to conduct and regulate our lives in the light of God's Word.

Therefore, walking by sight means to conduct our lives based on what strikes the eyes, what is exposed to our view or external appearance. It takes much more than the confession of faith to walk by faith genuinely. We must be resolved ardently in our hearts, with a conviction that what goes out of the mouth of God will not return to Him void (see Isaiah 55:10-11). His Word will accomplish that which God pleases, and prosper in the purpose for which it was sent.

MAKING THE IMPOSSIBLE POSSIBLE

. . . .

"And a certain woman, which had an issue of blood twelve years, And had suffered many things of many physicians, and had spent all that she had, and was nothing bettered, but rather grew worse, When she had heard of Jesus, came in the press behind, and touched his garment. For she said, 'If I may touch but his clothes, I shall be whole.' And straightway the fountain of her blood was dried up; and she felt in her body that she was healed of that plague" (Mark 5:25-29).

"And, behold, a woman, which was diseased with an issue of blood twelve years, came behind him, and touched the hem of his garment" (Matthew 9:20).

The situation of this woman in the above text was an impossible situation. She had an infirmity that in today's vocabulary would be termed as a terminal or a chronic disease, and her condition was distressful. The Scripture lets us understand that this woman had bled for twelve years without any medical solution. She had tried everything possible but to no avail. We all have issues in our lives for which we may have sought all that there is, but the problems stare us in the face and declare, "It is impossible." To God be the Glory, for we serve the Almighty God who specializes in turning impossibilities into possibilities.

What was this woman's infirmity? Her infirmity was an issue of blood. **What is your infirmity?** The Greek word used for *"issue of blood"* is called *Haimorrheo* (Strong's G131). It is a compound word comprising *Haima* (Strong's G129), meaning "blood," and *Rheo* (Strong's G4482) meaning "to flow." Haimorrheo, therefore, means "to suffer from a flow of blood," "to have a discharge of blood," or "to lose blood," from which the English word *"hemorrhage"* is obtained, which signifies "to suffer from a flow of blood." I need to let you understand the agony with which this woman had to grapple.

She had an issue of blood for twelve years: the Scripture declares in Leviticus 17:11 that "...the life of the flesh is in the blood..." This, therefore, means that when she was losing blood, she was being deprived of life in her flesh, she was losing strength, and was emaciating. Unbelievably real, she must have lost her structure over the period of twelve years beyond the point of recognition. This must have been a traumatic experience for her. She became a misfit socially, economically impoverished, and stigmatized by her infirmity.

She suffered many things of many physicians: this implies that her ailment caused her to suffer many things at the hands of many physicians. She could have been used for various kinds of tests, while both quacks and real physicians worked on her. They could have used her to test their new medical findings, or she could have become a study case for undergraduate interns.

She spent all that she had: this implies that she became poverty-stricken; selling everything she ever worked for or possibly had inherited. The infirmity ruined her financially.

Her case grew worse: the physicians had tried all that they could do and had given up on her. The woman did all that she was able to do and spent all she could afford, but she grew worse, with no hope of recovering. This became a dream from which she was never to awaken. She was now left at the mercy of her infirmity, which now was gradually eating into the fiber of her being.

The Scripture tells us that in her mess, she heard a message. What did she hear? Well, whatever she must have heard gave her hope in a hopeless situation, peace in the midst of confusion and despair. I believe she heard that Jesus Christ is the Messiah, the Savior of the world: that He walked upon the sea, healed the blind, raised the dead, cast out demons, cleansed the leper, and healed the disabled and that He was the Way, the Truth, the Life, and the Resurrection.

When she had heard all about Jesus, she concluded in her heart, "If I may but touch his garment, I shall be whole." In other words, she believed what she heard. For faith comes by hearing and hearing by the Word of God; she confessed the Word, for with your mouth is confession made unto salvation. She acted on the Word, for faith without works is dead (see James 2:20). No matter the circumstances or the mountains you are faced with, your impossibilities will become possible with God. Take time to hear, confess, and act on God's Word. For that which you understand and feed on will determine that which you will believe. That which you confess will determine your possession, and that which you act upon will decide your ultimate results.

WHAT COULD HAVE STOPPED HER MIRACLE?

The crowd roundabout Jesus Christ could have stopped her miracle. This was evident in her determination to receive her healing miracle. To see the multitude roundabout Jesus was another reality that she had to face.

- *Discouragement and disappointments*: She had tried everything at her disposal, to no avail. She could have been discouraged and disappointed to go on or unwilling to try something new.
- *Having bled for such a long time, she had no strength to push her way through*: This would have been a significant hindrance to her miracle. For she could have concluded that there was no point trying to walk her way through to where Jesus Christ was due to her physical and mental weakness.
- *The reports of man and physicians*: Holding on to the reports of a man and the physicians, rehearsing it and allowing it to echo in her mind, could have aborted her determination to believe in her miracle.

- *The people's opinion of her situation*: What people thought about her situation and how they evaluated it could have stopped her from receiving the miracle she so desperately needed.

The enemy's strategies have not changed, so we must heed the warning of God's Word *"Lest Satan should get an advantage of us: for we are not ignorant of his devices"* (2 Corinthians 2:11). You must be prepared to see beyond and overcome all of these hindrances, limitations, and much more than the enemy can and will bring against you in your quest for a miraculous breakthrough as it concerns your body, family, finances, businesses, and of course, ministry.

THE PLACE OF GOD'S WORD

"Let the words of my mouth, and the meditation of my heart, be acceptable in thy sight, O LORD, my strength, and my redeemer" (Psalms 19:14).

"But what saith it? The word is nigh thee, even in thy mouth, and in thy heart: that is, the word of faith, which we preach;" (Romans 10:8).

The Psalmist declares, let the *"words"* of my *"mouth"* and the *"meditation"* of my *"heart,"* be acceptable to you, implying that there is a connection, a link, between the words of our mouths and the meditations of our hearts. When the words of our mouths agree with the meditations of our hearts, there will be total results. We often don't receive or obtain the desired results because of disharmony and disconnection between the words of our mouths and the meditations of our hearts.

This is what the Scripture means when it declares that out of the abundance of the heart the mouth speaks, not just what is in your heart, but the excess of what is in your heart, which of course is the result of your thoughts and what you choose to meditate. God's Word is to be found in our *"mouth"* and *"heart."* The mouth speaks what is in the heart.

The ninth verse of the above chapter declares, *"That if thou shalt confess with thy mouth the Lord Jesus, and shalt believe in thine heart that God hath raised him from the dead, thou shalt be saved."* Often this verse is used in Christian meetings when leading the unsaved to Christ, which of course is not out of place. However, it should not be restricted only to the unsaved.

There are numerous benefits for the saved in that verse of Scripture. If what we confess with our mouths corresponds with what we believe in our hearts, it will affect us either positively or negatively. The words that we speak can put us above or beneath, give us life or death, make us failures or success, give us victory or defeat. We can become victors or victims; the choice is ours.

THE POWER CONFESSION – HOMOLOGIA

• •

"That if thou shalt confess with thy mouth the Lord Jesus, and shalt believe in thine heart that God hath raised him from the dead, thou shalt be saved. For with the heart man believeth unto righteousness; and with the mouth confession is made unto salvation" (Romans 10:9-10).

The Greek word for *"confess"* is *Homologéō* (Strong's G3670), and it is a compound word comprising *Homoû* (Strong's G3674), meaning "the same," and *Lógos* (Strong's G3056), meaning "something said," "to speak." Homologeo, therefore, means, "to speak the same thing as another," "to agree with" or "to acknowledge," to adopt the same style of speech, to speak alike. In our case, "homologia" means, *"saying the same thing God says,"* *"speaking according to His Word."*

If you confess with your mouth: this indicates speaking the same thing as another. Beware of this because you become what you confess. Hence, it is imperative that you must confess with your mouth what God's Word says about you. When you do that, you agree with God and His Word. To obtain results, you have to believe in your heart what your mouth confesses. The Scripture teaches that "...*out of the abundance of the heart the mouth speaketh*" (Matthew 12:34). Our mouths are the gateway to our hearts, therefore, whatever proceeds out of our mouth ought to be in harmony with what is in our hearts. A significant number of Christians are missing it by confessing with their mouths without necessarily believing with their hearts that God can do what He says He will do in His Word.

It is imperative, therefore, to know there is a connection between what proceeds out of our mouths and what we believe in our hearts. This combination works perfectly well as it achieves results. It is essential we understand that we ought not to look at the confession of God's Word as a "name it and claim it" formula, but we must confess God's Word in faith and trust that He will perfect all that concerns us (see Psalms 138:8). Above all else, we should know that confessing and agreeing with His Word pleases our Father God and should be our ultimate pursuit.

The Christian faith is called our confession. It is our open declaration of what we are in Christ Jesus, of what Christ is to us. Hebrews 3:1 teaches us that Jesus Christ is the Apostle and the High Priest of our profession while Hebrews 12:2 alludes to the same truth that Jesus Christ is the author and the finisher of our faith. The Greek word for "*author*" is *Archegos* (Strong's G747), meaning "a chief leader—author, captain prince." Therefore, Jesus is the chief leader—author, captain, prince— of our confession to the truth of God's Word.

This is so powerful that the enemy does not want us to gain access to this truth. The reason our confession of faith in God's Word is so powerful and produces extraordinary results is undeniably that Jesus Christ is the author, captain, prince and will see to it that our confession of faith produces outstanding and earth-shaking testimonies to God's glory.

It is vital that we take our confession of faith in God and His Word over our lives, families, ministries, enterprises seriously. It is a confession of what God the Father has done for us in Christ, our place in Christ Jesus, and our redemptive covenant privileges. Our Lord Jesus as the Apostle and High Priest of our confession guarantees and ensures that our confession of faith in God's Word is efficacious.

Discouraged or Encouraged, Your Choice

· ·

"Have not I commanded thee? Be strong and of a good courage; be not afraid, neither be thou dismayed: for the LORD thy God is with thee whithersoever thou goest" (Joshua 1:9).

The events that transpire in our lives are not always encouraging and can sometimes be devastating. In such moments, you have to choose whether to allow those circumstances to overwhelm or discourage you or to be encouraged and empowered, knowing that He that has begun a good work in you will bring it to fruition (see Philippians 1:6). If you wish to stay afloat in any daunting situation, you must yield to the admonition of Scripture in Philippians 2:5 that says, *"Let this mind be in you, which was also in Christ Jesus:"*

That is, you need to have the same attitude that Jesus had in the face of trouble. The account of Jesus calming the storm in Mark 4:35-41 revealed his attitude in the face of imminent danger and very terrified were the disciples. Jesus simply rose up and rebuked the storm. This is the attitude we should emulate when we go through the storms of life.

By God's Word, your outlook on the situation will determine the choice you will make. The example of David in 1 Samuel 30:6 states that *"...David was greatly distressed; for the people spake of stoning him, because the soul of all the people was grieved, every man for his sons and his daughters: but David encouraged himself in the LORD his God."* Nothing was encouraging in this situation but pain, anger, and hopelessness.

The circumstance that David and his army found themselves in was so devastating that the men wept until they had no more strength to cry and were so disheartened to the point of wanting to stone David. In this dilemma, even at the risk of losing his life, David encouraged himself in the Lord. I believe what made the difference is that he knew the counsel of God's Word as the final authority.

Don't Quit

. . . .

"Let us hold fast the profession of our faith without wavering; (for he is faithful that promised)" (Hebrews 10:23).

"Let us hold fast the confession of our hope without wavering, for He who promised is faithful" (New King James Version, Hebrews 10:23).

You are possibly on the verge of giving up on God, on yourself, and on everything that you have thought or believed in because of the events that have transpired in your life. I strongly admonish you not to quit, for the Scriptures encourage us to hold fast the confession of our faith. We are to be consistent in speaking the same thing as God's Word, and agree with and acknowledge Him in all things. The profession of your faith says you are healed, you are delivered, you are the head and not the tail, you are a success and not a failure, and your going out and your coming in shall be blessed; that is, the Lord shall preserve you in all your ways (see Psalms 91:11). Let me remind you of the Scripture that says that He (God) can *"...do exceedingly, abundantly above all that we ask or think, according to the power worketh in us"* (Ephesians 3:20).

The word *"able"* is the Hebrew word *Yakol* (Strong's H3201) which means "to be able, to have power, having the capacity to prevail or succeed," while the Greek word *Dynamai* (Strong's G1410) means "to be able, to have power whether by virtue of one's ability and resources, to be able to do something, to be capable, strong and powerful." Understand that God has the ability, the resources, the might, and the power to bring to fruition all that concerns you even when you don't. Knowing and experiencing the ability of Jehovah will cause you to hold on regardless of the circumstance.

CHAPTER 13

GOD'S WORD BRINGS CHANGE

"The entrance of thy words giveth light; it giveth understanding unto the simple" (Psalms 119:130).

"The entrance and unfolding of Your words give light; their unfolding gives understanding (discernment and comprehension) to the simple" (Amplified Bible, Classic Edition Psalms 119:130).

God's Word brings about changes that are impossible for anyone or anything else to achieve. It is imperative to reiterate that God's Word never changes but it changes things. For this simple reason, we must submit to the total counsel of God's Word as the final authority for our lives individually and collectively as a people. These changes could be drastic, instantaneous or spontaneous, or simultaneous. However, in whatever manner these changes occur, we must rest assured that the Word will come to pass although it may tarry.

At the entrance of God's Word, there is light. In other words, God's Word brings illumination and clarity to every aspect of our human existence. The light of God's Word will be experienced as we hear and yield to its promptings. We know that darkness is not just the absence of light, but darkness exists whenever and wherever evil is present and manifests its activities. The Scriptures declare in John 1:5 that "...light shineth in darkness; and the darkness comprehended it not." When the Word of God comes into your life, the light of His glory manifests in every aspect of your life, dispelling anything that is contrary to the will of God for you.

AT YOUR WORD

. . . .

"Now when he had left speaking, he said unto Simon, 'Launch out into the deep, and let down your nets for a draught.' And Simon answering said unto him, 'Master we have toiled all the night, and have taken nothing: nevertheless at thy word I will let down the net'" (Luke 5:4-5).

The Scriptures show us that multitudes pressed about Jesus to hear the Word of God, and after He was through preaching and teaching God's Word, He spoke a command to Simon, whose boat He had used as His podium to minister, saying *'Launch out into the deep and let down your nets for a draught.'* This simple command was to change the fisherman's frustration and disappointment after he had toiled all the night for fish to no avail.

Simon's response to Jesus was parallel to what the Master had commanded because at the time of Jesus' command, the natural circumstances were not favorable to the command that He gave. Another fact was that Simon and his colleagues had labored tirelessly through the night and were exhausted and disappointed for lack of results.

It was also evident that it was the wrong time of the day to catch fish and of course, these men were trained, skilled, and seasoned fishers. It would have seemed ridiculous as Jesus Christ, the son of a carpenter, who to them scarcely knew anything about fishing, asked them to launch into the deep for a draught. However, Simon in all of his confusion and frustration overlooked the opinions of the other fishermen present who considered it impossible that they would catch anything, and said: "nevertheless at thy *word* I will let down the net."

The word "nevertheless" signifies that he would have said in himself "nothing else is prompting me to do this as I have examined all the possibilities and none are to our advantage, but at your *word*, I will act with my confidence based on your command." As everything in the natural seems bleak and impossible and all hope seems to have been lost, remember that there is a word in the heart of the King of Kings concerning that situation. In spite of their condition, they caught fish at the words of Jesus. This shows that God's Word is alive and active, efficient, and true. Nevertheless!

However high the mountains or low the valleys, let God's Word be your rearguard and your confidence, for the Scriptures declare, "*...he spake, and it was done; he commanded, and it stood fast*" (Psalms 33:9). If our attitude is like that of Simon and we merely obey and act upon God's Word, irrespective of the cares and issues of life, we will experience changes in our lives.

Our father of faith, Abraham, had a situation of infertility, which he much desired to change, but that change could not have been brought about by human efforts. In Genesis 15, God spoke to him that He would make him a father of many nations, but at the time this Word was pronounced, it did not seem as if what He promised would ever come to fulfilment. However, when the time came, nothing could stop it from happening.

> *"And the LORD visited Sarah as he had said, and the LORD did unto Sarah as he had spoken. For Sarah conceived, and bare Abraham a son in his old age, at the set time of which God had spoken to him"*(Genesis 21:1-2).

POWER OF THE SPOKEN WORD

. . . .

"Jesus saith unto him, Rise, take up thy bed, and walk. And immediately the man was made whole, and took up his bed, and walked: and on the same day was the Sabbath" (John 5:8-9).

Jesus here in the text above addressed the lame man at the pool of Bethesda and said to the lame man, "Pick up your bed and walk" and immediately was healed and made by the spoken word. The spoken Word of God will bring about tremendous changes in every area of our human existence, for it possesses inherent power to bring it to pass. The Scripture lets us understand that *"A man's belly shall be satisfied with the fruit of his mouth; and with the increase of his lips shall he be filled. Death and life are in the power of the tongue: and they that love it shall eat the fruit thereof"* (Proverbs 18:20–21).

It is imperative for you to understand that you can do a great deal of good, or a great deal of hurt, both to others and to yourself, according to the use you make of your tongue (see James 3:5-6). This is because the words we speak wield great power either positively or negatively. As an example in the story of the fig tree demonstrates just how important words are; a word from Jesus produces dramatic results (see Matthew 21:18-22).

As the disciples journeyed with Jesus across the sea one day, while He was asleep in the lower chambers of the ship, there arose a tempest against them which caused the disciples to be so terrified that they actually told Jesus that He did not care if they perished as they could not understand how He could be sleeping through such a severe storm. All that Jesus did was to rebuke the storm by a Word fitly spoken, and it ceased (see Mark 4:37-39).

The Word Prevails

"So mightily grew the word of God and prevailed" (Acts 19:20).

The Word of God had such potency that, it prevailed over every circumstance and situation to the point that men were willing to give up their practices of idolatry and destroy their curious arts to follow Jesus Christ and this Word still does today (see Acts 19:19). As the Word of God grew mightily, it prevailed. God's Word increased, and the power of God was manifest as demonstrated by the extraordinary deeds that were wrought in and through the lives of the apostles. It suffices to mean that as we exercise and allow God's Word to grow in our lives, it will produce such power that the Word will prevail over our lives, will, emotions, and affections. It will overcome and reign over all of the schemes and onslaught of the enemy.

THE POWER OF GOD'S PROMISE

. . . .

"For as the rain cometh down, and the snow from heaven, and returneth not thither, but watereth the earth, and maketh it bring forth and bud, that it may give seed to the sower, and bread to the eater: So shall my word be that goeth forth out of my mouth: it shall not return unto me void, but it shall accomplish that which I please, and it shall prosper in the thing whereto I sent it" (Isaiah 55:10-11).

Hebrews 6:13 declares *"...when God made a promise to Abraham because he could swear by no greater, he sware by himself."* As we examine Abraham's life, it is evident that because of the issue that was pending in his heart, a particular outlook was formed but that changed at the evidence of a Word of promise from God. I know many people can relate to Abraham and Sarah as they are experiencing issues in their lives' journeys. This tends to affect their outlook on life, but when we can locate a word of promise from God's Word, it changes our outlook on life and eventually determines our conduct in the midst of seeming chaos.

It becomes imperative to know that God made a promise and swore to bring that promise to fruition despite the circumstances. This is one of the fundamental truths that we, as children of God, must grasp - the certainty that God's Word is our ultimate guarantee. Understand, child of God, that God's Word is His promise and His will. Unlike man, God fulfills what He promises. He is not a man that He should lie or need to repent. The power to activate and accomplish His Word is built on the promise. Hallelujah.

God gave us His Word and designed it to work in every area of life. God's Word works, and time or distance does not limit it. As you consistently put your confidence in God's Word, it will put to shame the works of darkness and release the ability of God on your behalf, which will resolve your concerns.

CHAPTER 14

OBEDIENCE TO GOD'S WORD IS KEY TO GODLY LIVING

"Ye shall walk after the LORD your God, and fear him, and keep his commandments, and obey his voice, and ye shall serve him, and cleave unto him" (Deuteronomy 13:4).

OBEDIENCE DEFINED

In the above passage of Scripture, the Greek word translated *"Obedience"* is *Hypakouō* (Strong's G5218), a compound word that comprises *Hypó* (Strong's G5259), meaning *"Under"* and *Akoúō* (Strong's G191), meaning *"to hear."* Hypakoúō, therefore, implies to hear under (as a subordinate), i.e., to listen attentively; by implication, to submit, to obey, to heed or conform to a command or authority, be obedient to. The Hebrew word for obedience is often translated "to hear." Genuine hearing includes obedience.

God speaks, and the faithful response is to hear and respond accordingly.

Obedience is "the act of obeying, or the state of being obedient; compliance with that which is required by authority; subjection to rightful restraint or control" (Webster's Revised Unabridged Dictionary 1913). Obedience is the willingness to submit to the authority of another and to do what one is asked or told to do, whether it is in response to God or a human being. It is also the positive, active response to what a person hears. Obedience, therefore, entails "to observe, to do, to keep, and to heed."

OBEDIENCE TO GOD

In the Scriptures, obedience is used mostly in the sense of submission to God's Word, His will, and His commands. God expects obedience from us as His children. We are commanded to obey in the preceding Scriptural text. We are also advised to obey because obedience is better than sacrifice. However, with these warnings, we are often susceptible to disobedience, which eventually is to our detriment.

To obey means to hear and positively heed or respond accordingly. Hence, it is imperative to understand that obedience is not perfected without a positive response. Apostle James in his epistle states that you should be a doer of the Word and not a hearer only, which is indicative of obedience being in active response to God's Word (see James 1:22-25).

OBEDIENCE, KEY TO GODLY LIVING

"This book of the law shall not depart out of thy mouth; but thou shalt meditate therein day and night, that thou mayest observe to do according to all that is written therein: for then thou shalt make thy way

prosperous, and then thou shalt have good success"
(Joshua 1:8).

Here, you see Joshua, who after the death of his master
was entrusted with the leadership of the children of Israel, an
enormous assignment and a task beyond his capabilities. However,
God saw and still sees beyond human frailties. After God had
communicated His purpose to Joshua and what He would have him
do, He gave him the instruction that would ensure the successful
accomplishment of his God-given assignment and endeavors. This
instruction was for him to observe, that is, "be obedient," to God's
instructions, which would, of course, determine whether he would
prosper in his ways or not.

Consequently, obedience to God's Word is a vital key to living
a godly and victorious life. It is, therefore, very crucial for you to
fulfill the will of God and your prophetic destinies in this season
like never before. It is one thing to hear or read God's Word, but
also you must take heed of the Word. Obedience to God's Word
was one of the most significant demands of God to the patriarchs
of old, His chosen people, and is still His demand for you today.

> *"And the LORD God commanded the man, saying, 'Of
> every tree of the garden thou mayest freely eat: But of
> the tree of the knowledge of good and evil, thou shalt
> not eat of it: for in the day that thou eatest thereof
> thou shalt surely die'"* (Genesis 2:16-17).

After the Lord had created man, He placed him in the Garden
of Eden and gave him a command to eat of every tree in the garden,
except the tree of the knowledge of good and evil. It is important to
know that God made provision for man's welfare, which included
all that was necessary for him to enjoy and live a godly life. God
gave a command to Adam to dress and keep the garden, that is,
to cultivate and guard the garden against intruders. However, he
failed in keeping the garden from the most destructive intruder,
the devil.

Allowing the intrusion of the enemy and accommodating his lies sabotaged man's obedience to God's Word, and the same is true for many Believers today. Obedience brings blessing, but disobedience allows curses to operate in your life (see Deuteronomy 11:27-28).

If the enemy and his lies are unrestrained, obedience to God's Word, which was and still is the key to living a godly life and enjoying the fullness of God, will be sabotaged. The drama of how your first parents disobeyed God's command (His Word) and the consequences no doubt reveals to you the inevitable aftermath awaiting whomever is caught in this web of satanic manipulation.

The Scripture declares in Genesis 3:1-3 that *"Now the serpent was more subtle than any beast of the field which the LORD God had made. And he said unto the woman, Yea, hath God said, Ye shall not eat of every tree of the garden? And the woman said unto the serpent, We may eat of the fruit of the trees of the garden: But of the fruit of the tree which is in the midst of the garden, God hath said, Ye shall not eat of it, neither shall ye touch it, lest ye die."* God expressly told Adam that the day he ate of the tree of knowledge of good and evil he would *"surely die."* It is imperative that you understand that when Adam ate of the tree, he did not die physically, in the sense that he no longer existed as it were, but died spiritually, being cut off from the source of his livelihood.

This indicates that when you disobey or go contrary to God's Word, you cease to experience and enjoy an unbroken relationship with God. Whenever a man violates God and His Word, he stops enjoying the fruit of God's provision and instead lives by the fruit of his labor or the work of his hand, as was the case with Adam. It is conclusively clear that disobedience cuts us from God's divine supply.

What the enemy did then and still does now is attack God's Word and cast doubt in your mind, causing you to be uncertain and question the integrity of God's Word, which ultimately results in disobedience to God's Word. This suffices to mean that to walk in obedience to God and His Word, you need to protect your heart and mind through the knowledge of God's Word, prayers and godly thoughts against the corrupt influences that are everywhere in our world, the lies and pollutions of the enemy (see Proverbs 4:23).

OBEDIENCE TO GOD RELEASES BLESSINGS

. . . .

"And it shall come to pass, if thou shalt hearken diligently unto the voice of the LORD thy God, to observe and to do all his commandments which I command thee this day, that the LORD thy God will set thee on high above all nations of the earth: And all these blessings shall come on thee, and overtake thee, if thou shalt hearken unto the voice of the LORD thy God" (Deuteronomy 28:1-2).

Obedience to God's Word brings you to that place of never-ending relationship with God, where the miraculous is released into your life as you submit and take heed to God's Word. From time immemorial, we see the pattern that God continuously employs in bringing His people into the realm of the miraculous, causing them to experience His manifold blessings.

In Genesis 12:1-3, God asked Abraham to leave his land of nativity, his parents, siblings, and everything that he possessed and migrate to a land that was to be shown to him. God said that He would make out of him a great nation, bless him, and make his name great, such that he would become a blessing. Abraham obeyed without objection.

As Abraham stepped out in obedience to God and His Word, he experienced the mighty hand of God. It is, therefore, evident that the degree to which you experience the miraculous release of the blessings of God is relative to the degree to which you are obedient to God's Word.

Apostle Paul emphasizes in Ephesians 1:3-6, *"Blessed be the God and Father of our Lord Jesus Christ, who hath blessed us with all spiritual blessings in the heavenly places in Christ: According as he hath chosen us in him before the foundation of the world, that we should be holy and without blame before him in love: Having predestinated us unto the adoption of children by Jesus Christ to himself, according to the good pleasure of his will, To the praise of the glory of his grace, wherein he hath made us accepted in the beloved."* Over the years, I have seen many loving Christians confess this verse of Scripture day and night without enjoying the fruits thereof. It is certain that this is God's Word and it should be confessed alongside other verses of Scriptures in the Bible.

However, people can become extremely frustrated with continuously confessing that they shall receive spiritual blessings, but not seeing the manifestation of these blessings in the physical. I firmly believe that you do not need the blessings only in heavenly places, but in the physical, here on earth, and one of the most essential and vital ways to bring them into our realm is through obedience to God's Word.

Apostle Paul explains, *"For this cause also thank we God without ceasing, because, when ye received the word of God which ye heard of us, ye received it not as the word of men, but as it is in truth, the word of God, which effectually worketh also in you that believe"* (1 Thessalonians 2:13). When you take God's Word literally for what it says and let it reign over your circumstances, then its supernatural power is released to work in your life.

Moses declares in the book of Deuteronomy 30:16 that for you to live, multiply, and enjoy the blessings of the Lord, you must obey His commands, statutes, and judgments. Obedience is the key to enjoying the fullness of God spiritually and physically. The consequences of disobeying God's Word are so devastating that it would be a tragedy to disobey God. The blessings that result from obeying God are too numerous and beneficial to be overlooked. Understand, however, that obedience is not so much about what you can obtain from God as it is about honor, love, and reverence.

OBEDIENCE TO GOD KEY TO OVERFLOWING ANOINTING

. . . .

"And we are his witnesses of these things; and so is also the Holy Ghost, whom God hath given to them that obey him" (Acts 5:32).

Given the importance of the anointing in our personal and professional lives, it's imperative that we understand and define what it is. The Hebrew word for *"anointing"* is *Mâshach* meaning 'to rub with oil,' 'to consecrate' while there are many Greek words that describe the anointing as "to anoint with oil", "to cover with oil; first to rub inside, then to apply as you rub" "to anoint with oil in order to set apart for something specific." Consequently, the anointing of the Holy Spirit is the supernatural enablement of the Holy Spirit to function and the fulfillment of God-given assignments.

Obedience is one of the keys to walking in the anointing of the Holy Spirit. The anointing of the Holy Spirit is the endowment of supernatural abilities that enable you to function in His Kingdom. For that reason, to experience and operate in the anointing, obedience to God and His Word must, inevitably, be a priority. It is important to reiterate that the degree to which you will walk in the anointing is directly relevant to the degree to which you are in obedience.

The anointing guarantees victory. It is crucial to understand that as the ages get darker compared to past generations, the need for the believer to walk in the anointing of the Holy Spirit becomes more and more pertinent. It is, therefore, vital to maintain a high level of the anointing by walking in obedience to God and His Word. From the ages past, we have seen this as the primary key that determined how the patriarchs of old walked in the anointing or lost the anointing in their walk with God.

The story of Samson is a reminiscence of one of the men of old that experienced the overflow of the anointing of God when he

147

stayed obedient to the commands of the Lord (see Judges 13-16). He also is an example of one of the men that lost the anointing and experienced a significant fall as he walked in disobedience to God's commands. Experiencing the overflowing power of God comes with a price and great responsibility. Obedience to God and His Word is a definite prerequisite for the overflow of the power of God operative in a man's life.

OBEDIENCE TO GOD'S WORD IS
KEY TO SPIRITUAL SIGHT

. . . .

"The man answered and said unto them, 'Why herein is a marvellous thing, that ye know not from whence he is, and yet he hath opened mine eyes. Now we know that God heareth not sinners: but if any man be a worshipper of God, and doeth his will, him he heareth. Since the world began was it not heard that any man opened the eyes of one that was born blind. If this man were not of God, he could do nothing.' They answered and said unto him, 'Thou wast altogether born in sins, and dost thou teach us?' And they cast him out. Jesus heard that they had cast him out; and when he had found him, he said unto him, 'Dost thou believe on the Son of God?' He answered and said, 'Who is he, Lord, that I might believe on him?' And Jesus said unto him, 'Thou hast both seen him, and it is he that talketh with thee.' And he said, 'Lord, I believe. And he worshipped him.' And Jesus said,' For judgment I am come into this world, that they which see not might see; and that they which see might be made blind'" (John 9:30-39)

It is incumbent on the believer to obey God's Word. Not only did the blind man believe Jesus' Word, but he also obeyed His

Word. The ways to a satisfied life in Christ are contained within God's Word to you.

Consequently, you must come to the understanding that it is not just enough to hear the Word. There are times when obedience to God's Word may seem unrealistic, absurd, or burdensome. However, to have access to the anointing and the blessings that come as a result of the anointing, you must learn to obey in spite of what you think.

The story of Naaman, the Syrian, who had leprosy, is an example of obedience to God's Word when it is not convenient. The command given to him did not make sense to him and, of course, his status and prestige were in the way. He had been informed that a mighty prophet of God in Israel could show him how to be healed, but when he got to Elisha's house, Elisha didn't even come out to talk to him. Instead, he sent his servant with a message, "Go, wash seven times in the Jordan, and your flesh will be restored, and you will be cleansed" (New International Version, 2 Kings 5:10). Naaman became very angry but eventually did as he was told to receive his healing. There was no shortcut as God is no respecter of persons.

HOW DOES OBEDIENCE TO GOD AFFECT YOU?

Most people do not understand the concept of obedience and consequently take it for granted that lack of obedience does affect their spiritual walk with God, and this cannot be further from the truth. Let us now examine how obedience affects your spiritual walk.

Obedience Is Essential for Worship

"And Samuel said, 'Hath the LORD as great delight in burnt offerings and sacrifices, as in obeying the

voice of the LORD? Behold, to obey is better than sacrifice, and to hearken than the fat of rams'" (1 Samuel 15:22).

Genuine and authentic worship is not in burnt offerings and sacrifices as clearly stated in the above Scriptural text. You can only offer worship that pleases your Father when you are walking in obedience and submission to His will. Obedience to God is a significant concept for you to enter into the realm of total victory. Obedience, therefore, is of great consequence, and it is the litmus test for real and genuine worship. As a result, obedience to God and His Word is of the utmost importance in your walk with Him. Furthermore, John 4:23-24 states that true worshipers shall worship the Father in spirit and in truth. There is no way that you can worship in truth and spirit without being obedient to Him.

Obedience of Faith Brings about Salvation

"For as by one man's disobedience many were made sinners, so by the obedience of one shall many be made righteous" (Romans 5:19)

Without obedience to God and a profession of faith, salvation cannot become a reality for you. If you hear the gospel preached and do not move in obedience to that which you hear, and accept it by faith, the salvation that God graciously provides through His Son, Jesus Christ, will elude you. Apostle Paul declares in Romans 10:16, "But they have not all obeyed the gospel. For Esaias saith, 'Lord, who hath believed our report?'" You are required to obey the gospel as it does affect your spiritual walk, and the Scriptures reveal, "Take heed unto thyself, and unto the doctrine; continue in them: for in doing this thou shalt both save thyself and them that hear thee" (1 Timothy 4:16).

Obedience Secures God's Blessings

"And all these blessings shall come on thee, and overtake thee, if thou shalt hearken unto the voice of the LORD thy God" (Deuteronomy 28:2)

"If they obey and serve him, they shall spend their days in prosperity, and their years in pleasures" (Job 36:11).

Obedience to God and His Word for you secures spiritual and material blessings. Scriptures are littered with men and women who enjoyed divine blessings as a result of walking in obedience. Equally, you'll see others that were subjected to curses because of their disobedience. Moses, the man that God used to deliver the Israelites from bondage, had to overcome his fear of speaking, and his insecurities obeyed God during his encounter at the burning bush. He then went on to become the impressive leader of the Israelites as they migrated from bondage into the land of promise (see Hebrews 11:24-29 and Exodus 3:1-17).

CHAPTER 15

GOD'S WORD
FOREVER SETTLED

"Forever, O LORD, thy word is settled in heaven"
(Psalms 119:89).

"My covenant will I not break, nor alter the thing that is gone out of my lips" (Psalms 89:34).

"My covenant I will not violate, Nor will I alter the utterance of My lips" (New American Standard Bible, Psalms 89:34).

"I won't break my agreement or go back on my word" (Contemporary English Version, Psalms 89:34).

In the text above, the word *"settle"* is the Hebrew word *Nâtsab* (Strong's H5324), which means, "to be firmly fixed," "established": that is, the Word of God is firmly fixed and established in Heaven. Therefore, the Word of God concerning you and your loved ones before the foundations of time is firmly set and established in Heaven. Nothing can alter its purpose. Everything else in life can fail you as a person, a family, a Church, or a nation, but God's Word will not fail you. Child of God, understand that this is not wishful or positive thinking, but an unwavering assurance of God's Word. God's Word is your eternal guarantee that all He has purposed and ordained before the beginning of time for you will be manifest. God's Word is not to be treated as the word of man, for His Word is His covenant with us, and He will not alter the Word that has gone out of His mouth. It is important to note that ignorance of God's Word, the covenant provision in the believer's life, is equivalent to an eventual shipwreck of his/her faith.

> "(As it is written, I have made thee a father of many nations,) before him whom he believed, even God, who quickeneth the dead, and calleth those things which be not as though they were. Who against hope believed in hope, that he might become the father of many nations, according to that which was spoken, 'So shall thy seed be.' And being not weak in faith, he considered not his own body now dead, when he was about an hundred years old, neither yet the deadness of Sarah's womb: He staggered not at the promise of God through unbelief; but was strong in faith, giving glory to God; And being fully persuaded that, what he had promised, he was able also to perform" (Romans 4:17- 21).

> "He was fully convinced that God is able to do whatever he promises" (New Living Translation, Romans 4:21).

The Greek word for "fully persuaded" is Plērophoréō (Strong's G4135), which means "to be proved fully, brought to an end and entirely accomplished or to be confirmed with the fullest evidence." In other words, Abraham had the confirmation in his heart, entirely convinced that God was able to do what He said as fully evidenced in God's Word, irrespective of the prevailing circumstances as he had yet to see the physical evidence of the promise. The Apostle Paul here speaks of Abraham, the father of faith, who could not have a child with his wife, Sarah. The Almighty God spoke and promised Abraham, having complained of his childless situation and considering that at this time, he and his wife had gone past the age of childbearing. Medically speaking, it was impossible because the man was advanced in age and the woman had passed the age of menopause.

Hear me, children of God, no matter how challenging the situation you may be going through might seem, it can never intimidate God. Count it all joy, my brethren, for one word from Him will turn your nightmares into moments of joy and testimonies. God spoke to Abraham and told him that he was going to have a child, and his descendants were going to be great. You need to understand that it was impossible as far as man's reasoning was concerned, but with God, all things are possible (see Matthew 19:26). Abraham received the Word of the Lord, not considering the circumstances, being fully persuaded that what He had promised, He was able to do.

GOD'S WORD VERSUS CIRCUMSTANCES

Apostle Paul admonishes you to study the Word of God, showing *"thyself approved unto God, a workman that needeth not to be ashamed, rightly dividing the word of truth"* (2 Timothy 2:15). The unfavorable circumstances in our lives and how we react and respond to them will, very often, contradict God's Word, oppose all He has said and can become the archenemies of our faith in God's Word. You have to understand that your circumstances can never invalidate God's Word over your life.

Whenever you allow situations and circumstances to overrule God's Word, you deny yourself of the promises of God's Word and its prevailing power. At that moment, you begin to walk in unbelief just as the Israelites did when they heard the reports of the men they sent to spy out the Promised Land; you must remember that God hastens *"[his] word to perform it"* (Jeremiah 1:12). God declares in Isaiah 55:11, *"So shall my word be that goeth forth out of my mouth:* [concerning all that concerns you - spiritually and physically]: *it shall not return unto me void, but it shall accomplish that which I please, and it shall prosper in the thing whereto I sent it."* The eternal word of God will always prevail against your circumstances, as a result, put your trust and confidence in God's unfailing Word to deliver on its promises.

GOD'S WORD HIGHLY MAGNIFIED

. . . .

"I will worship toward thy holy temple, and praise thy name for thy lovingkindness and for thy truth: for thou hast magnified thy word above all thy name" (Psalms 138:2).

"I bow before your holy Temple as I worship. I praise your name for your unfailing love and faithfulness; for your promises are backed by all the honor of your name" (New Living Translation, Psalms 138:2).

To magnify means, "to declare and show forth one's glory and greatness, to increase one's esteem, reputation and authority." The New Living Translation declares that all the honor of His name backs the promises of God. This signifies that God has announced and shown forth the glory and greatness of His Word and vouches for it with the honor and majesty of His name. The Word of God cannot be separated from Him, and His reputation and authority guarantee whatever He has said, so it will come to fruition.

It is laudable to reiterate that God has highly magnified and backed up His Word by all the honor of His Name. This is indicative of the seriousness of what I am talking about and reveals, beyond any doubt, the potency that God's Word possesses. Well, like the average child of God is ignorant of this *timeless truth* and this explains why they sometimes find themselves running from pillar to post in search of fulfillment and solutions to their problems in life outside of what He has spoken.

God will not allow His name to be dragged in the mud, so every Word that He said must be accomplished to His glory, as long as you commit to obedience. The Word of God is, therefore, the final arbiter of your life, and it possesses undeniable potency to accomplish its purposes and plans just as God has ordained.

TWO IMMUTABLE THINGS

. . . .

"I have sworn by myself, the word is gone out of my mouth in righteousness, and shall not return, That unto me every knee shall bow, every tongue shall swear" (Isaiah 45:23).

The Scripture declares, *"Wherein God, willing more abundantly to shew unto the heirs of promise the **immutability of his counsel,** confirmed it by an oath: That by two immutable things, in which it was **impossible for God to lie,** we might have a strong consolation, who have fled for refuge to lay hold upon the hope set before us:"* (Hebrews 6:17-18).

God made a promise to Abraham, and because He could not swear by anyone greater, He swore by Himself. The Hebrew word for *"swear"* is *shaba* (Strong's H7650), which implies "to swear, to give one's word, to bind oneself with an oath." While the Greek word for *oath* is *hórkos* (Strong's G3727), meaning, "that which has been pledged or promised with an oath, to affirm, promise or threaten with an oath, in swearing to call a person or thing as a witness." The preceding text, therefore, implies that God completely bound Himself with an oath and called Himself as a witness to what He promised.

Child of God, the Lord desires to reveal to you the immutability of His counsel (His unchangeable will, purpose) for your life, and He has confirmed it by two immutable things that make it impossible for God to lie. God's Word declares that by these

157

two immutable things, it's impossible for the Almighty God to lie or deny the heirs of promise of what He has purposed to do or accomplish in your life. This implies that if God said He was going to heal you, deliver you, bless, and protect you that Word is undoubtedly guaranteed and cannot change.

What are these two immutable things? They are (a) **God's Word (Promise),** and (b) **God's Oath.** When God made a promise to Abraham, He did not only speak but took an oath to confirm His words, as a guarantee and seal of what He had said. On a human level, to keep a promise that, in any case, humans rarely adhere to, you swear by the greater, which to you is a confirmation and an end to strife. However, God could not swear by any greater or lesser, for heaven is His habitation and the earth is His footstool.

My God, there was none beside Him, neither was there any above Him. Therefore, Jehovah took an oath upon Himself and declared, "I am and I will." Child of God, since God does not and cannot lie, and He is all-powerful, He will fulfill all of His Word. The unchanging nature of God and His Word is the believers' comfort and confidence that these two immutable things secure your destiny as dictated by God.

Beloved, it has been the ignorance of God's Word about your healing, prosperity, holiness, deliverance, and inheritance that has robbed you for this long. I dare you to get into God's Word for yourself, discover and take hold of the promises of God, appropriate them for yourself, confess them, and claim them by faith today, for they are yours to be possessed. Glory be to God!

TRUTH VERSUS FACTS

"Then said Jesus to those Jews which believed on him, 'If ye continue in my word, then are ye my disciples indeed; And ye shall know the truth, and the truth shall make you free'" (John 8: 31-32).

Do you live according to the truth or facts? Are you governed by your circumstances or are you standing on God's Word? You see, the truth is not subject to change, but facts are. Truth is based on God's Word and not on circumstantial evidence. Facts are based on circumstantial evidence and not on God's Word. For example, it is a *fact* that you are poor or sick, but the **truth** is that He became poor that you might be rich and you are healed by the stripes that were laid on Jesus Christ.

It is imperative, therefore, to understand what God's Word says about you and all that concerns you. God's Word about you is the truth and what the doctors or circumstances declare is factual and therefore subject to change at any given point in time. In Jeremiah 29:11, the Scripture states unequivocally that the thoughts of God toward you are of peace, and not of evil, with a definite purpose to bring you to an expected end. That is His plans and intentions for your life will ultimately come to fruition and prevail over the works of the enemy.

In effect, sickness, diseases, and poverty are not your portion and not in the will of God for your life. In this world now where everything is unstable with wars and rumors of war on every side and significant technological advancement, human development is still unable to respond to the issues that plague humanity. It is, therefore, conforming as it was in the past as well as today that you need a higher source of power to depend on at all times, and this can only be the unchanging and uncompromising Word of God, your guarantee.

THERE SHALL BE A PERFORMANCE

. . . .

"Then said Mary unto the angel, 'How shall this be, seeing I know not a man?' And the angel answered and said unto her, 'The Holy Ghost shall come upon thee, and the power of the Highest shall overshadow thee: therefore also that holy thing which shall be

born of thee shall be called the Son of God'" (Luke
1:34-35).

There was a young virgin girl in the land of Judah betrothed
to a young man by the name of Joseph. This young woman had a
visitation one day from an angel with a message that she was to
bear a child who would be the Savior of the world. This kind of
news should have been anticipated and appreciated by any young
woman, but there were just numerous concerns - she knew no
man, everyone would think she had stepped out on Joseph or that
she and Joseph had sinned. Her reputation was at stake so she
would have some apprehensions from this. This made the very
message more absurd and unbelievable as far as her finite mind
was concerned. This would be considered a reasonable reaction by
any human being as giving birth to a child requires a biological
father and mother.

The message of the angel overwhelmed her so much that she
had to ask how this thing would be done since she had not known
any man. The angel told her how the Holy Ghost would come upon
her and the power of the Highest (God) would overshadow her. As
if the initial news was not mind-blowing enough, the angel gave
her further news that Elizabeth, her cousin and a woman who had
been called barren, had in her old age conceived a son. This was a
testimony given to Mary as confirmation that "with God nothing
is impossible" (Luke 1:36; Matthew 19:26).

Mary finally caught the revelation of the sovereignty and
omnipotence of God, and it gave her the courage to line up with the
Word of God, causing her to make a declaration of faith saying, "...
*be it done unto to me according to thy word.' And the angel departed
from her"* (Luke 1:38b). *"And blessed is she that believed: for there
shall be a performance of those things which were told her from the
Lord"* (Luke 1:45). The Greek word for *"performance"* is *Teleiosis*
(Strong's G5050), which denotes a "fulfillment," or "completion,"
or "perfection," or "an end accomplished as the effect of a process"
or "an event which verifies the promise."

With the announcement to Mary that her aged cousin who had been barren for years was with child, she left straightaway to see her. On her arrival, something extraordinary took place. As soon as Elizabeth heard the salutation of Mary, the baby in her womb leaped for joy and Elizabeth, as she was filled with the Holy Spirit, began to prophesy and speak into Mary's life, declaring that there shall be a *performance* of those things that were spoken of the Lord (see Luke 1:41-45).

In other words, there should be fulfillment, completion, of that which the Lord had spoken to her. Child of God, you must understand that no matter what the condition or situation you may face in life can be, you must take advantage of God's Word and discover what it says about you, for there shall be a performance of God's Word if only you can believe.

God's Word is your ultimate guarantee.

LIVING STONE WORLD WORSHIP CENTRE
"One God, One Family, One Destiny"
A.k.a. NEW CREATION LIFE MINISTRIES

Living Stone World Worship Centre "One God, One Family, One Destiny" (a.k.a.) New Creation Life Ministries, is a ministry fully committed to reaching the unconverted in our world with the Gospel of reconciliation.

Since the unconverted abound outside the sanctuary, the Gospel has to be taken to wherever they are to fulfill the command of God; preach the good news to the ends of the earth.

Our aspiration is to fulfil the call and command of God which is the Great Commission: *"Go ye therefore, and teach all nations, baptizing them in the name of the Father, and of the Son, and of the Holy Ghost: Teaching them to observe all things whatsoever I have commanded you: and, lo, I am with you always, even unto the end of the world. Amen"* (Matthew 28: 19-20).

This mandate from God to build and establish the foundation of lives by holding forth the word of life, preaching the word of faith, and demonstrating the power of the Holy Spirit will be pursued and accomplished through:

- Church planting
- Seminars/conventions
- School of disciples
- Living Stone World Outreach
- Leadership training

Our Vision is built upon, pursued, and organized around seven simple concepts to ensure consistency and balance. We call them the Pillars of Vision.

PILLARS OF VISION

· ·

- Identifying with God's love and purpose for all
- Identifying with and maintaining the integrity of God's Word
- Identifying with the work and leading of the Holy Spirit
- Identifying prayer, praise, and worship as a way of life
- Identifying ministerial gift and God's plan for equipping the saints for the work of the ministry
- Identifying with God's plan for global evangelism, our supreme task (our mission)
- Identifying with His message and His life walk (discipleship)

We are committed to reaching you with the unchanging love and the burden-removing, yoke-destroying power of God.

KINGDOM COVENANT PARTNER

L iving Stone World Worship Centre, "One God One Family, One Destiny" a.k.a. New Creation Life Ministries is a ministry that is on the cutting edge of what God is doing in these last days.

> *"But thou shalt remember the LORD thy God: for it is he that giveth thee power to get wealth, that he may establish his **covenant** which he sware unto thy fathers, as it is this day"* (Deuteronomy 8:18).

The Scripture makes us understand that the only purpose in the heart of God when He gave us the power to obtain wealth was and is to enable us to become partners in establishing the covenant, which He swore to our fathers.

With this piece of truth, I sincerely enjoin you to rise to the purpose for which you have been empowered by becoming a covenant partner spiritually and financially today.

Your prayer and financial support will bless and enable someone to hear the gospel of our Lord Jesus Christ.

To request your free no-obligation KINGDOME COVENANT PARTNERS' information, please contact:

Living Stone World Worship Centre
"One God, One Family, One Destiny"
A.k.a. New Creation Life Ministries
P.O. Box 30
1200 Brussels
Belgium
E-mail: apostle@livingstoneworld.org
Websites: www.livingstoneworld.org

ABOUT THE AUTHOR

D r. Richard ONEBAMOI is an apostle by divine calling, an author, a business consultant, a leadership alignment strategist, and a success facilitator. Dr. Onebamoi is the founder and senior pastor of Living Stone World Worship Centre, "One God, One family, One Destiny," located in Brussels, Belgium. Dr. Onebamoi is also a certified coach, speaker, and trainer for The John Maxwell Team. Furthermore, he is the Founder of Men of Visionary Excellence (M.O.V.E).

Dr. Onebamoi is the founder and executive facilitator of The ROCK Consulting Group, with a mandate to inspire your performance, expand your imagination, cultivate your dreams, empower your success, and help you discover, develop, and maximize your God-given potential. He can provide leadership, success motivation, and educational and positive personal development training that will maximize potentials and minimize liabilities.

A vibrant and charismatic minister and highly sought after conference speaker and published author of several books, including *Success Power Points, Kingdom Principles on Leadership, Whose Report Will You Believe?, Anatomy Of Frustration,* and *Winning Ways for Success.* Dr. Onebamoi carries an apostolic grace upon his life, an anointing to bring changes to the lives of his listeners. He has a profound and unique insight into God's word. As he ministers around the globe, God continually marks his ministry with the demonstration of the Holy Spirit, transforming lives by the Word of His power.

Dr. Onebamoi is happily married to Catherine K. ONEBAMOI, who co-pastors with him and the associate executive facilitator of The ROCK Consulting Group and Richard Onebamoi International (ROI). They are blessed with four children, Naomi-Lisha, Nearia-Destinie, Nathania-Mia, and Nathan-Richard Jr., and they reside in Brussels, Belgium in the heart of the European Union.

You can contact Richard for speaking in churches, seminars, and conventions at:

Richard Onebamoi
P.O. Box 30
1200 Brussels
Belgium
Email: info@richardonebamoi.com
Website: www.richardonebamoi.com

www.ingramcontent.com/pod-product-compliance
Lightning Source LLC
LaVergne TN
LVHW011327080426
835513LV00006B/228